THE HOW-TO GUIDE TO LAWYERING LIKE LINCOLN

The How-to Guide to Lawyering like Lincoln
"Lessons, Tips, and Tales on Practicing Law and Hanging out a Shingle"

Michael J. Dunn

Editing: Mylene Ladan
Typesetting and cover design: Anita Jovanovic

Published by:

Vandeplas Publishing, LLC – March 2016

801 International Parkway, 5th Floor
Lake Mary, FL. 32746
USA

www.vandeplaspublishing.com

ISBN 978-1-60042-277-5

THE HOW-TO GUIDE TO LAWYERING LIKE LINCOLN

*"Lessons, Tips, and Tales on Practicing Law
and Hanging out a Shingle"*

MICHAEL J. DUNN

Mike Dunn has been an attorney for nearly 30 years. He received his bachelor of science degree in business administration from Elmhurst College, his masters of business administration from Western Michigan University, and his juris doctor from the John Marshall Law School in Chicago. He was an associate professor and clinical director of the Access to Justice Clinic at Western Michigan University's Thomas M. Cooley Law School, where he currently is an adjunct professor of law teaching courses that include: *Transition to Law Practice, Children and the Law, Criminal Practice, Child Abuse and Neglect, Moot Court, Pretrial Practice* and various assorted street lawyer classes. He is a co-host of the marginally syndicated weekly radio legal talk show *The Lawyer's Show* based in Grand Rapids, Michigan and played throughout Western Michigan. He maintains a busy law practice and has tried cases in state and federal court in Michigan, Wisconsin, and Illinois. He has published several legal periodicals on the *Lawyer as Entrepreneur* and the *Teaching of Law* and a chapter or two in practice manuals for the State of Michigan. He is also a frequent lecturer at the Michigan Supreme Court Abuse and Neglect Appellate training, Juvenile Justice Forums at Grand Valley State University, and at Aquinas College's Olin School.

Mike can be reached at attorneymikedunn.com, dunnm@cooley.edu, mdunnlaw@aol.com, or on Facebook at Attorney Michael Dunn.

DEDICATION

To The Vigorous Defender of Lost Causes

TABLE OF CONTENTS

PART III

MUST DO!

PART I

Who Knew?

INTRODUCTION:

LEGAL EDUCATION AND THE STATE OF LAWYERING

So, here is what you are told: *Law school is too expensive and not worth it. There are too many lawyers, and only a few are working. You have to be from a top-tier law school to even have a shot at a career.*

This is just plain B.S.

Of course, law school is expensive. It is not like brain surgery, where you get a signing bonus when you become board-certified and where you can easily pay off your student loans when you get a job with a surgical practice. It is, however, as Abraham Lincoln once said, *an honest calling.*

Let's examine this concept of going to law school and whether it is a reasonable decision. First, there is the undergraduate degree. It is a requirement, but it should not be one. I believe that three years of hard foundation and two years of law school should be sufficient. And the blows-against-the-empire part of me says that half of law school should be what they call pedagogical (I hate that pompous word) and the other half practical. There, I've said it. I don't want to dumb law school down, I want to practical it up. It is a good, solid career choice and should be treated as such. Law school has become a three-year course in taking the bar, and that should not be the case. The argument would be that the top of the top schools, the Harvards and Stanfords and Michigans of this world, have not fallen prey to this dastardly game, and they may be right, but I was a B to A- student in college, not an AAA student who got in the ninety-ninth percentile on the LSAT.

Let's face it: law school is a fancy trade school, an expensive trade school, and a grueling trade school. It is not, however, like becoming an electrician. You will never get your hands dirty, and you will never electrocute yourself—unless you do it on purpose. The practice of law is a time-honored and dignified profession that will not only survive but thrive in a changing world

So, where are we now? We are not at a crossroads where lawyers become extinct. Take accountants. What if we start a flat tax system where everyone pays a 20% sales tax on everything and there are no other taxes? Do you actually think there will be no need for accountants? Hell, no! Even with what Amazon did to retail, people did not stop buying. They just started buying things differently. Amazon was just a disrupter of the status quo. They were just buying using a different model. Law school and lawyering is in transition to a different model.

I would guess you are thinking that would mean sending our legal work offshore to India, to marginally-trained or even well-trained lawyer equivalents. Maybe that is a small part of the change. The big part is the delivery of service. Look at your jar of peanut butter. I'll wait while you get one. Are you back? OK. What has Big Peanut Butter done to this jar? It has repackaged it into tiny, bite-sized, carry-along, one-serving containers that allow the company to charge 10 times what they were charging for half as much peanut butter because you are now buying a more convenient life. Bingo! There it is: packaging. What, after all, is McDonalds? They sell hamburgers. How hard is it to make a hamburger? It is about as hard as boiling water. They market, package, re-market and repackage, and BAM, they have a billion dollar product made out of a simple item that everybody wants. We do not need hamburgers, but we do need to eat, and McDonalds makes us want their hamburger. Get it? Legal services are just that, legal services.

The days of the highly perfumed barrister may be over. The big firm lawyer is fast becoming the hang-out-the-shingle-hometown lawyer. It is a change that says that people want service, not just brains. They want handholding, not pedagogy. A good lawyer is going to become part of that reawakening of the house-call doctor. The one who answers the phone at midnight with the panicking parent on the other line saying, "What shall I do, my baby was arrested for drunk driving. Please get him out of jail." Now, the answer to this is "let him sleep it off, and he will be out in the morning first thing when his alcohol breath test registers 0." What you are really saying is that you also do not have any control over getting someone out in the middle of the night, BUT, and this is a really big but, the client wants to know what this is all about. Your value, and this should always be a free call that pays legal case-karma later, is to educate and counsel. That is why we are often referred to as attorneys and counselors-at-law.

The future successful lawyer is one who is ready to put clients first instead of money. This will be the wave of the future. It is back to basics all over again. What does a good basketball coach do with his fancy players? He makes them do laps, lay-ups, and free throws until they turn blue. They can do all the slam-dunk stuff during a game, but not at practice. You are going to have to simply make your way into a career. This requires ignoring the crowd of naysayers. This requires trips to a jail to visit a client, who has no hope of getting out, just because you are caring enough to sit and talk for a minute to let him know that you are there.

The path starts in college. Students ask me all the time what major they should take. This is a no-brainer: Take a major that will make you better rounded. Take a major that emphasizes writing and reading, and more writing and more reading, throw in some public speaking, and you are gold. I would suggest English as a major or medieval history over pre-law or law enforcement any day. There is no such thing in my book as pre-law. You are in college to expand your mind, so expand it with the abilities that would make you a good lawyer. Writing is #1. Even though the real goal of many lawyers is to stand in court and dazzle the jury, much like the basketball slam-dunk, the problem with this is that it forgets the basics. The courtroom performance will come many years after the love and torture of rigorous education turns into savvy and wisdom.

Remember, law school is not like undergrad. It does not teach you law but how to analyze law. It is not about memorizing definitions— I still remember that the rule of perpetuities has something to do with: an action must vest, if it vests at all, within 21 years plus a live in being, but I digress. It is about learning a new way to think, not a new way to memorize. The best memory of anyone I ever knew in law school was a student named Frank. Frank could memorize pages of material. Ask him about the ruling in *Palsgraf,* and he could tell it to you verbatim. But ask him how to apply it to a given situation, and he was lost. That, my friend, is fatal, and it was for him. Law school is not supposed to be a three-year bar review course. Law school should teach you quickly whether your skills allow for the mega-monster test at the end of the tunnel.

Let the silk-stocking firms continue to recruit from Harvard at starting salaries three times what the rest of us mortals make. Let the Cravaths of this world have a 10-year partnership track where you are pretty assured you will be a millionaire but also that you will need to cherish work over family and billable hours over a life. Law is a job. It is a good job, and as Abraham Lincoln said, it is an honest calling. But, as Lincoln also said, while his passion was politics, he fed his family by being a lawyer. It is a simple equation.

As Brian Dirck wrote in *Lincoln the Lawyer,* p. 165: *"Mr. Lincoln was comfortable in the law. He was in his element on the circuit, acting the part of a 'poke-easy' in his office, or putting on one of his well-calculated performances before a jury. In all of the secondhand accounts of Lincoln's legal career left behind by colleagues', not one hints that Lincoln felt dissatisfaction with his job. He went elsewhere – the statehouse, Congress, and eventually the White House – to feed his ambition. But he used the courthouse to feed his family, and maybe to feed some part of himself, to find a degree of personal security unavailable elsewhere."*

There is no question that the state of legal education and of lawyering is changing, and has done so for a long time, especially since Lincoln's time. If you have the appetite for success and the stomach for uncertainty, becoming a lawyer is the place to be. If you want a guaranteed income, stay out of solo practice. It has its ups and downs. This is not to say it is not profitable. A wrongful death case helped me build a summer home. The money is there. The big firms are bloated and slowly crumbling away from the time-honored tradition of "Bill! Bill! Bill!" What is left is you and I: We are not the last of a breed, but change is our bright future. It is a grand future filled with accomplishment and independence. Notice that Lincoln thought that being a lawyer provided a *degree of personal security unavailable elsewhere*. This is completely true. Even after nearly 30 years of practice, I still, at times, wake up and smile and feel so accomplished in being the master of my own fate.

I do believe that none of us actually know what it is to have a career until we are knee-deep in it. So, what we do, according to the world, is that we create avenues to endeavors. The barriers to entry tell the tale as to how hard or easy the path will be to become part of the 'club.' A brain surgeon has four years undergrad, four years medical school, a residency and on and on. Ten to twelve years later, she is a brain surgeon, truly. The education required to become a brain surgeon is a high bar and a huge barrier to entry. The greater the barrier, as the MBA theory goes, the higher the pay. It just feels good to have a juris doctor degree. I tell students all the time that this license in my wallet says that I have a career, a career that not just anyone can do. Unlike Lincoln who 'read' for his right to be a lawyer, I (and you) had to go through four years of undergrad, three years of law school, and the test from hell. Only after all this can I hang out a shingle or join the fraternity of an honest calling.

When I first graduated from high school, I wanted nothing, really, to do with school. I hated high school and basically won the award for missing the most days of any student in my school's history and still graduate in four years. It was so bad that one morning, I was awoken by a knock on my bedroom door. It was my guidance counselor telling me I needed to go to school. It turns out that my mother had left the key in the mailbox so he could get into the house. Junior college allowed me to smoke in the classrooms and think deep thoughts. The only deep thought I had was trying to construct a path of least resistance to finishing at least a two-year degree. I am not saying I was in a simple program in junior college, but my math book had a picture of Snoopy in it. 'Nuff said.

So, there I was in my twenties wanting to find easy ways to make big money. Geeze, there is always a first: someone wanting to make it big with little skin in the game. I am here to announce, maybe for the first time, that it ain't possible. The end.

Here is what is possible: anything you put your mind to and strive at all times to excel to complete. I went from a marginal C in high school to solid Bs, in college and I even got straight As in law school at one point. All because I learned there are no easy answers and no shortcuts.

It is a long haul, but it pays off in the end. So, do not let all the negative talk and thoughts interfere and, as they say in the gym shoe biz: JUST DO IT!

DISCUSSION QUESTIONS

1. Why did Lincoln call being a lawyer 'an honest calling'?

2. Do you think three years of law school is needed?

3. Should law school be a combination of pedagogical study and practice preparation? Should these be in equal proportions? How would you design the perfect requirement for a law degree? Remember, Lincoln never went to law school. He 'read' for the law. Being a lawyer was done through an apprenticeship system rather than

through the completion of a degree. It was all about practice and self-study. Consider this while designing the requirements to become a lawyer.

4. Do you agree or disagree that the 'big firm' model is dying'? If so, what will replace it?

5. How important do you think solo practice will be in the future?

6. How would you design a service-oriented law practice?

CHAPTER 1

LINCOLN WAS A STREET LAWYER

Lincoln: *"The [law office] furniture, somewhat dilapidated, consisted of one small desk and a table, a sofa or lounge with a raised head at one end, and a half-dozen plain wooden chairs. The floor was never scrubbed.... Over the desk a few shelves had been enclosed; this was the office bookcase holding a set of Blackstone, Kent's Commentaries, Chitty's Pleadings, and a few other books. A fine law library was in the Capitol building across the street to which the attorneys of the place had access."*

Abraham Lincoln was a self-taught jack-of-all-trades. He attended law school for less than a year and then was admitted to practice in Illinois based on a certificate he had procured from the court of an Illinois county certifying his "good moral character." He swore under oath to "faithfully execute the duties as attorney and counselor." He basically read his day's version of Black's Law Dictionary and became the president.

From that point on, Lincoln practiced law with a partner in Springfield, Illinois. He was known as a lawyer with an impeccable gift for oral argument, and his argumentative skills far surpassed his legal research skills. When you add to this his uncanny ability to simplify and abbreviate complex legal cases, as well as his ability to read juries, you will see that he was truly exceptional.

Lincoln was a street lawyer. A street lawyer is a 'do everything that comes in the door' lawyer. He did a steady stream of both criminal and civil. Most of his cases, however, were contract disputes and debt collection issues.

Lincoln began his career partnering with Mary Lincoln's cousin, Stephen Logan. They rented the third floor of a new building on 6th and Adams Streets in Springfield. The federal government had the first floor for the post office, and the second floor was occupied by the federal court. At the time, in 1840, it was the only federal court in Illinois. Lincoln and Logan dissolved their partnership in 1844, and Lincoln took William H. Herndon as his junior partner.

Lincoln's proximity to the court is one of the first great lessons in building a practice (more on this later). I spent my career less than a block from the state courthouse and two blocks from the federal courthouse. Why? Because you have to go where the lawyering is. Certainly, you can open a practice on Mars, if you like, but the concentration of work or the Zen of the business is the hub where the courts are. Period. You also have the concept of people believing that the 'big shot' lawyers, if there is such a thing, are downtown. Downtown can mean almost anything, but it usually means where the court is.

On a typical day in the life of a new lawyer, you will find and see lawyers everywhere as you walk from your car to the office. You may walk to lunch and see lawyers, and on and on. Why do you want to be around lawyers, you may ask? The reason is simple: They practice law. Throughout my career, I have been stopped on the street by some newbie asking, "Do I need to file a default before I can file a summary judgment motion on a collection action?" I may or may not know the answer, but the lawyer will never leave my presence without knowing how to find the answer or who to call— most likely, another downtown lawyer. Without the near constant contact of lawyers around you, especially if you are a solo, the silence is deafening. You need input, and the more comfortable you are around many lawyers, the better.

Starting my own practice as a street lawyer and with these clients was a godsend. They were clients who were either odd ducks or clients who could not pay the enormous bills that the firm could deal out. I remember one partner telling me, "We have to charge $10,000 to wrestle a file to the ground." This meant getting up to speed on a file. For the same work, I would charge a few hours of time. The big firm would pass it around to the associates and para-professionals, and then the partner would bill to read their underlings' summaries.

After leaving a big firm after three years, I finally started to meet the local attorneys. At one of the first meet-and-greets over beers, one of the lawyers said, "I make x amount of dollars per year being on my own." He was not bragging; it was more by way of helping out a new lawyer. I thought that was certainly a take home number. He paused and said, "Not a bad gross." In my first year, I made twice what he was making. It really hit home. I learned that night the most important lesson as a lawyer: PLAY YOUR OWN GAME. Do not worry about what other lawyers are doing or how well or badly they are doing. There is competition everywhere. This is the Zen of law practice. Just practice. Focus on the work, and the money will take care of itself. The end.

Twice a year, Lincoln traveled the Eighth Judicial Circuit. This included as many as 14 counties. There they went, with a small group of attorneys and a judge, Lincoln traveled to the various county seats to try any case that was ready. This was like making house calls. The court system would go to the county seat, complete with a judge and lawyers at the ready. In essence they brought the court to the people. They traveled from town to town by horseback and spent a few days in each town they passed to resolve whatever issues they could.

Lincoln's fees were usually in the $5 to $20 range, but he once charged $5,000 for a single case. Lincoln represented the Illinois Central Railroad throughout the 1850s, and he charged his largest fee ever for a case he won for the railroad. It was called *Illinois Central Railroad v. McLean County*. The Illinois Central Railroad owned 118 acres of land in McLean County, Illinois, and the county assessor levied a tax of $428.57 on the railroad's property. The railroad argued that the Illinois General Assembly Act incorporating the railroad exempted it from taxes. The railroad hired Lincoln and sued McLean County to stop the county from selling railroad land to pay taxes. The parties reached an agreement, and the bill was dismissed. Lincoln received $5,000 for his legal services—but he had to sue the railroad to collect his money.

In 1861, when Lincoln was about to depart from Springfield and travel to the White House, he pointed to the sign hanging from his law office. It said "Lincoln and Herndon." He told Herndon, "Let it hang there undisturbed." He promised Herndon that should he return to Springfield after his term, they would go right on practicing law "as if nothing had ever happened."

From a Law Lecture by Lincoln:

I am not an accomplished lawyer. I find quite as much material for a lecture in those points wherein I have failed, as in those wherein I have been moderately successful. The leading rule for the lawyer, as for the man of every other calling, is diligence. Leave nothing for to-morrow which can be done to-day. Never let your correspondence fall behind. Whatever piece of business you have in hand, before stopping, do all the labor pertaining to it which can then be done. When you bring a common-law suit, if you have the facts for doing so, write the declaration at once. If a law point be involved, examine the books, and note the authority you rely on upon the declaration itself, where you are sure to find it when wanted. The same of defenses and pleas. In business not likely to be litigated,---ordinary collection cases, foreclosures, partitions, and the like,---make all examinations of titles, and note them, and even draft orders and decrees in advance. This course has a triple advantage; it avoids omissions and neglect, saves your labor when once done, performs the labor out of court when you have leisure, rather than in court when you have not. Extemporaneous speaking should be practised and culti-vated. It is the lawyer's avenue to the public. However able and faithful he may be in other respects, people are slow to bring him business if he cannot make a speech. And yet there is not a more fatal error to young lawyers than relying too much on speech-making. If any one, upon his rare powers of speaking, shall claim an exemption from the drudgery of the law, his case is a failure in advance.

Discourage litigation. Persuade your neighbors to compromise whenever you can. Point out to them how the nominal winner is often a real loser---in fees, expenses, and waste of time. As a peacemaker the lawyer has a superior opportunity of being a good man. There will still be business enough.

Never stir up litigation. A worse man can scarcely be found than one who does this. Who can be more nearly a fiend than he who habitually overhauls the register of deeds in search of defects in titles, whereon to stir up strife, and put money in his pocket? A moral tone ought to be infused into the profession which should drive such men out of it.

The matter of fees is important, far beyond the mere question of bread and butter involved. Properly attended to, fuller justice is done to both lawyer and client. An exorbitant fee should never be claimed. As a general rule never take your whole fee in advance, nor any more than a small retainer. When fully paid beforehand, you are more than a common mortal if you can feel the same interest in the case, as if something was still in prospect for you, as well as for your client. And when you lack interest in the case the job will very likely lack skill and diligence in the performance. Settle the amount of fee and take a note in advance. Then you will feel that you are working for something, and you are sure to do your work faithfully and well. Never sell a fee note---at least not before the consideration service is performed. It leads to negligence and dishonesty---negligence by losing interest in the case, and dishonesty in refusing to refund when you have allowed the consideration to fail.

There is a vague popular belief that lawyers are necessarily dishonest. I say vague, because when we consider to what extent confidence and honors are reposed in and conferred upon lawyers by the people, it appears improbable that their impression of dishonesty is very distinct and vivid. Yet the impression is common, almost universal. Let no young man choosing the law for a calling for a moment yield to the popular

belief---resolve to be honest at all events; and if in your own judgment
you cannot be an honest lawyer, resolve to be honest without being a
lawyer. Choose some other occupation, rather than one in the choosing of
which you do, in advance, consent to be a knave.

Legal scholar Mark E. Steiner wrote: "Abraham Lincoln was not a diligent student of the law, but when pressed by necessity, he was a sophisticated user of the available sources of legal information. His early legal training and the rapid changes in antebellum law ensured that his legal education continued throughout his law career. Although Lincoln advised would-be lawyers to 'still keep reading' after becoming licensed, Lincoln's reading instead was directed toward the case before him."

DISCUSSION QUESTIONS

1. What does being a street lawyer mean to you? What did it mean to Lincoln? Is a street lawyer just a lawyer who is a jack-of-all-trades or does it mean a bit more?

2. Why is it a good idea to practice where the court and lawyers are?

3. What does charging $10,000 to wrestle a file to the ground mean? Is this a good or bad thing? If you work with big clients and big cases, doesn't it talk all that to feel comfortable on a case?

4. Learn to play your own game. Why is this good or bad?

5. Discuss why Lincoln probably had to fight to get his $5000 in the Illinois Central case.

CHAPTER 2

LINCOLN LESSONS: THE BUSINESS OF LAW

Let's look at the previous chapter and parse out Lincoln's practice philosophy. First, his office was Spartan, and I do not mean filled with Michigan State memorabilia.

LESSON #1:

The [law office] furniture, somewhat dilapidated, consisted of one small desk and a table, a sofa or lounge with a raised head at one end, and a half-dozen plain wooden chairs.

I would take minor issue with the office, but little else. I believe the takeaway is that every penny you spend on furniture, you take out of your pocket. With that said, you must have a presentable space to make clients feel comfortable and to show that you have it all together, meaning, somewhat successful. Image is a whole lot when you are selling air. Doctors can fix your broken arm and make you feel better. A lawyer takes a problem and makes you feel less badly. You still feel bad after the lawyer leaves your life.

The image of the office goes hand in hand with the image of dress. Other quotes from Lincoln suggest that although he was thought of as sloppily dressed, he was not. He wore his finest to court and when attending to clients.

There is a solo practitioner down the hall from me in the same building. I can see through the window as I walk the halls to the exit the way he has it set up. He uses an actual gym locker for coats and another for files. He uses garage furniture materials for storage that he has painstakingly refinished. His desk is an old front door that he also finished and put legs on. He has a metal rolling library stand to hold books and files. On the bottom is his printer and paper. I would guess he spent $100 for everything in the office, and I am writing about it in a book. I think it looks awesome and is super clever. When clients come in, they will have the take away that this lawyer is frugal and super clever. This is the lawyer you want working on your case.

Now, you can also look like you are sitting in a junk pile to some people. There is the time-honored view of lawyer's leather, the big roll top desk, and the leather-bound books. This works for some, especially those of us who are a bit older.

LESSON #2

Over the desk, a few shelves had been enclosed; this was the office bookcase holding a set of Blackstone, Kent's Commentaries, Chitty's Pleadings, and a few other books. A fine law library was in the Capitol building across the street to which the attorneys of the place had access.

This mindset is the key to a profitable practice. Don't buy books or subscribe to expensive services. Learn to utilize the local library, law school, or college for your legal research. I will say over and over that you can use ICLE (Institute of Continuing Legal Education) books on 'Basic Practice' and a few specialty ICLE books on 'Drunk Driving' or 'Wills and Trusts,' but that is it.

It is clear that legal research with actual books is becoming a relic. The only thing you will need is paper statutes and court rules for your day-to-day practice. Everything beyond that is going to be Internet-based anyway. You know you can search any Supreme Court case you want. Sign into any state database, and you will have forms for days. Join a list on 'Children and the Law,' and hundreds of specialists will tell you how and where to get everything from law review articles to free treatises. It is all in the Internet. Spend your time and money on a good computer and printer rather than on building a library you once saw on 'My Cousin Vinny'. Books are now window dressing, and the best lawyers simply have an inexpensive subscription to a legal research product that younger lawyers or lawyers on a budget can go to the local library to use.

This is really not an issue anymore, but I do see law services that provide a monthly fee for instant access to law sources. I would skip those.

LESSON #3

Lincoln practiced law with a partner in Springfield Illinois for all of his legal career.

Lincoln always had a partner. As the story goes, he would ride the circuit (this is where the term "circuit court" came from), try dozens of cases around the counties in the state of Illinois and then come back and put half of his money on the table for his partner, who would do the same. Some months, he would have a lot to divide, and his partner would have little, and on and on. This was a true partnership, instead of the 'eat what you kill' model, which is the norm for what we call solo practice and/or office sharing. I am a solo practitioner. Presently, there are two other lawyers in my office. I pay rent. I keep ALL the rest of my money. But when the going's tough, I'm on my own. I guess the best way to have a long and fruitful career is to have a partner or two to ride out the bad weather.

When I talk about going solo or hanging out a shingle, I in no way mean being alone. That is a bad way to go. You need people in the next office or down the hall to bounce things off of. One of the lawyers I practice with has been practicing nearly 20 years, but we talk several times a week about the cases we have and the problems we are trying to solve. You can never strategize enough. Remember, lawyers are professional problem-solvers. Understand that first, and you will prosper.

If you work at a big firm, you know the practice of knocking on the door of a partner when you are an associate and asking the partner a question. First, questions are tricky. You run the risk of having the partner scratch his head after you leave and saying to himself, "how could we have hired such an idiot?" You could also get the atta boy look for catching a fire early. The best way to do it is to ask a contemporary or an associate who is not too busy eating his competition. Many times, you are given a mentor, and that person is assigned, charged, and directed to keep you alive.

The real purpose of doing it yourself and reinventing the wheel is so that you know how to do it. Slaving until midnight and writing off the time so you do not look addlepated is part of the practice. It is spending hours looking for a court rule that was right in front of your nose. I used to research till I was getting the same answer over and over. When this happens, you know you are done.

I have had senior partners in to talk to my class of new lawyers. First, they will say, "if I give you an assignment, I want it done within the timeframe I give you. I do not want it quick and wrong." *Quick and wrong*. These are brilliant words. Anyone can do the research licketysplit and hand it in fast to get that extra kudos. Well, that ain't the way it goes. First, the partner may have 100 projects going on and may not even look at yours for a month. The associate, on the other hand, sits in the office biting his nails and grinding his teeth, waiting for live or die approval which never seems to come. If the lawyer says anything about the project—and more often than not he will not remember—we are not kindergartners needing trophies and plaques, and he will compliment you by continuing to give you work. Get that and get it quick. The lawyers above you in the firm are YOUR CLIENTS, AND YOU HAVE TO TREAT THEM THAT WAY.

LESSON #4:

Lincoln's Law Office: *They rented the third floor of a newer building on 6th and Adams Streets in Springfield. The federal government had the first floor for the post office and the second was the federal court.*

All I can say to this is: BINGO!

They were in the same building as a court. Are you kidding me? Where do people go to see lawyers? At or near the court. Where do lawyers congregate? Near courts! It is as obvious as the nose on your face. It is romantic to move into the country to serve your peeps. I get it. I understand that. However, from a business perspective, you need to be in close proximity to the court system. In larger cities, you will find the state court, federal court, and even the court of appeals within several blocks of each other.

The argument that your clients do not want the hassle of parking downtown or do not like to drive into the big city can easily be solved. Go to their house. Be that country lawyer, but have an office with the city-folk because an even grander argument is that clients think the big-timers are downtown. Period. Think of it as going to a big city hospital as opposed to a country one. The perception is that the better doctors are there. Right or wrong, people believe this. Perception rules, especially when it comes to law office placement.

Here are the two office basics: 1. Be by the court and 2. Don't practice alone. Simple. This does not in any way mean your office has to be expensive. You just have to know the right people. If, for example, you asked people on a farm what to do to get a horse, they would say, "Hell, I can go to Charlie's and get one for free, he was just telling me that he has one too many." If you ask people who know nothing about horses how to get one, they will do an exhaustive search and come up with a multi-thousand cost estimate because they don't know a Charlie. You have to meet Charlies.

As I have said, and will say over and over, the very first place I rented was for $500 a month. It was centrally located and across and down the street from all the courthouses I could ever need. I found it by hanging around the local bar association and getting to know the people who worked there. The bar is a vital life link to your early beginnings. I learned vital lessons there, including that you are judged by whom you associate with. This is a truism we all know but can become prey to if we are not very careful and protective of that reputation we are sculpting.

LESSON #5:

Lincoln's fees were usually in the $5 to $20 range, but he once charged $5,000. He had to sue for the $5000.

The main lesson here is to be fair but firm and get your money upfront as often as you can. If you are a criminal defense lawyer, you will need to get as much upfront as possible. If your state allows it, this is a perfect line of work for the flat fee case. A drunk driving case can easily be a sum certain for a first, and another fee if it is a second, and so on. The beauty is you open and close the billing file—there is nothing to it. You do not need to be a collection attorney as well as an advocate. The reason you should get your money upfront in criminal law is obvious: the lawyer goes to lunch, and the client goes to jail.

If you can't do it flat, then charge a hefty retainer. A retainer is really a bill against fee. You have a bank account for your client that you use as you earn it. If you have a flat fee case, the money is yours. There are challenges to this if your fee ends up being considered unreasonable. Let's say that you charge $10,000 for a big case and then it is settled with a phone call. This would be unreasonable. There is the argument that your name and reputation caused the prosecutor to rethink his client's position—but not a $10,000 decision. A fee of $2500, based on what is called 'value billing' would be fair. Value billing is the excellent result of billing where you ring the bell but only charge a little. Many lawyers use this to pad the bill up based on the quality of the result.

This does not mean you can agree to a fee of $5000 and then send another $5000 bill when the case is dismissed. You must stick to your agreement.

As for the $5000 that Lincoln charged for litigation, besides it being a big-dollar case, it was also not an unusual result. Not getting paid a bunch, that is. The case made it all the way to the Supreme Court. The amount of work involved in getting to the Supreme Court, even back in Lincoln's time, is astronomical. The problem is when you hear the Court of Appeals or Supreme Court; this only means that you lost in a lower court. Client and loss go hand in hand. It is the nature of the beast. A full half of the time, someone loses. It is just the calculus that goes into lawsuits. And, with the math of the suit comes the inevitable let down client. This disappointment is always magnified when you charge a lot for attorney fees. There are two ways around this is: First, manage expectations from day #1, and, second, get your money upfront. Where have I heard that before? Managing expectations does not at all mean being pessimistic. You have to believe in the case, and you have to let your client feel comfortable in knowing that you are 'on-board.' You can, however, be very careful not to build up the possible outcome. The lawyer who says "we have a slam-dunk on our hands" is in for many rude awakenings.

The chances of having to sue a client for your fee is always there, but I discourage suing former clients. One lawyer I shared office space with always waited two years before he sued a client. Why wait two years? That's easy: it is the malpractice statute of limitations in my state. It happens all the time that people find something even more wrong with the case "you" lost after you sued them. It is like they are willing to let bygones be bygones for the loss until they have to pay for it. Going back to the 50/50 equation, every winner has a loser on the other side, and you have another equation that is stacked against a lawyer who got what the client perceives to be a bad result.

This is especially true in family law. I use the word 'family' to branch into divorce. Divorce, custody, support, and nonesuch are a loser's game. It ends in divorce. Get it? They get divorced, divided their stuff, and shuttle their children back and forth from one angry parent's house to the other. It is using the court system to break the contract they originally swore they never would. Standing in the back of the courtroom one day (I still the take time to do so just to watch for new tips and ideas), I saw the judge taking the 'pro/con,' a term we use to describe when jurisdictional language is put on the record, and at the very end, he said, "at the beginning, you walked down the aisle and you now end it walking down the aisle to the judges bench."

Divorce practice is an odd practice for the collection of money. It is filled with expensive lawyers who are more thespians than lawyers. Since the issues are all so personal to each family and each client wants to get the least bad result, it tends to draw showmanship, acting to convince your client you are performing well.

As a quick example, I submit:

I stood in the back of the courtroom and saw a rotund lawyer who looked from the back like Alfred Hitchcock. He had a cane with a gold handle, and he was leaning against the podium as if it was an accoutrement to his bow-tied suit lawyer uniform. He was flailing around and gaily spouting off to the judge words like "paramour" and "clandestine behavior." I looked to the front counsel tables where a friend of mine named Mary sat. I walked up to her while this verbal barrage was occurring and whispered into her ear. I said, "Mary, do you want absolute proof that Tom D. is nuts?" She smiled with approval. "Look around, there is no one in the courtroom but us, no client, no opposing party, and no audience." Tom D was just doing it because he could.

This is why you charge large retainers that you bill against, and when you are down to, say, half, you replenish and have that in a fee agreement. So, weekly or monthly, as you earn the time, you transfer the money you earned from your IOLTA account to your general account. The IOLTA or *interest on lawyers trust accounts* is a place you put unearned or undistributed client funds. It was originally designed to send the interest to bar associations to help fund worthy projects. In the past few years, with interest rates at rock bottom, little has been added to the fund. A word about IOLTAs: Never let it go into a negative balance. This is super bad. The state bar is flagged by the bank if you do. You will then have to explain what happened, take classes on how to manage a law practice, and get a grievance against you on your record.

So, what is the point about never suing clients? Unless it is for a large amount of money, most lawyers find it more trouble than it is worth. You have a client who has chosen not to pay, for whatever reason, and then you set them on fire by filing a suit? If they were mad to begin with, watch out. Just let it go, and let karma get 'em.

LESSON #6

Lincoln: *"Never let your correspondence fall behind."*

This would seem to be part of the diligence lesson, but it goes far beyond that. It is about papering your client or emailing them or making whatever smoke signal thing comes next. You are selling time. You are selling what is thought to be words, air and little else. How is a client to know if they have made good use of their money if you do not keep them well apprised?

Think about it this way: You have hired an attorney for a small criminal matter or a civil collection case or whatever. They paid you a down payment against your billing as a retainer. Let's say you get $2500 or even $5000. This is a whole lot of money from someone who makes $35,000 a year, or even for a parent who is paying for a child who makes nothing. What kind of investment are they making? Of course, they are paying for your expertise and your time. They want a resolution to the drunk driving case a child got into. They do not know the law or the judge, but they know they paid a hefty sum.

The only way you can make them feel like their interests are being served and that their money is well-spent is through correspondence. Letters are always welcome. Even the 'no news' letter that recognizes the fact that they exist counts. And what makes the 'no news' letter even better is when you send a bill at the end of the month that says

N/C (no charge) next to the entry about the letter. Lawyers are expensive, and you have to be considerate of the fact that clients want to pay but do not want to pay to be fleeced.

> Dear Divorce Client,
>
> I just wanted to drop you a note to tell you that we are in a holding pattern for the next two months. As you know, there is a six-month period until we can finalize the divorce. We have all our ducks in a row and are just waiting till we get closer to the five-month mark to send a settlement proposal to your wife's attorney. If we send one now, we will appear anxious, and that would not be advisable.
>
> I hope all is well. By the way, I saw your son made the All Star team at his school. Great work!
>
> Yours,
>
> *(Sign Mike, not formal)*
>
> Michael J. Dunn

This type of lawyering could be called 'hand-holding.' I call it an insurance policy. Only you can see and understand the train wreck that is up ahead in a divorce. There are so many hurt feelings and so much blame that goes around. Protect yourself by not ingratiating yourself with your client but by being a diligent machine working toward his best interests. It will serve you well and will soften the blow when he realizes that he once had twice as much stuff. Now, of course, you are always preparing for the inevitability of financial surgery. The problem is, and the legislature has it kind of right, that the necessary waiting period is a time of not just reflection, but an understanding of what you can't get your arms around from jump. In a divorce especially, but I would add any high-stakes litigation, there are five stages of grief:

denial, anger, bargaining, depression, and acceptance. It takes time to filter bad news into realization and, ultimately, the acceptance stage.

I cannot tell you how many stories I have heard about overbilling or failed communication. Neither puts you in the hall of fame of client service. Both can get you grieved, that dreaded hit to your reputation that ends up following you like that file from elementary school they said would follow you for your whole life.

One of my favorite federal judges speaks at seminars from time to time and opens with, "Write to your clients. Paper your files. It helps in client communication and helps outline the fact you did all you were asked to do when they file the 2255 (federal grievance) after they have been sentenced to 20 years in prison. Inevitably, they will file a grievance because the guy in the cell next to him did and they just copied it and filed it. With a complete file, you are basically bullet-proof."

The catch-up game is a loser's game. When you get behind, even in your calls, and, believe me there will be plenty, you fall into the 'I'm sorry' mode of operation. This is no place to be for a productive attorney. Rule number one is returning your calls every day. That means every day of the week (even weekends). When you are out of town or on vacation, find someone to leave a message that says you are out of town, but always leave an emergency way to get ahold of you if you do not have a legal assistant.

There are varying philosophies on this. Some lawyers do not want to be easily reached. One of the most popular criminal defense lawyers where I practice is unreachable. His phone is always full of messages to 'call back at another time'. Yet people find him. Why? Because he is the best around. Just ask him, and even he will tell you that. Other lawyers will also man a 24-hour help typeline to be available anytime. This is a bit too much but is better than the normal street lawyer having a 'full' inbox for messages. Being too accessible, especially if you bill every call, can get you into hot water with clients. My advice is to be available for return calls from 9-5 and just make calls after five if you have not returned all the calls that have come in during the day. Any new call after hours you can save till tomorrow.

To take this to the extreme and to show you that lawyers are first and foremost common sense problem-solvers (I already said I am limited on common sense, that is for MY problems, not yours; there I have tons). I received a call on Thanksgiving at around 3:00 p.m., when many people were sitting down to dinner. I left the room to be alone, and a man with a shaky voice said the following:

"You a lawyer?"

I responded, "Yes."

He then said, stammering, "I just stabbed my brother. What should I do?"

Now, let's look at that statement and remember that I was answering the phone on a holiday. Doesn't it strike you that that first call to me, a lawyer, was bordering on the absurd? I mean, the answer was so obvious, I almost couldn't stop myself from saying, *wouldn't you dial 911 first, you moron?* Be that as it may, I was able to stop myself.

He continued "I just stabbed him and do not know what to do."

I remember saying, "Is he hurt bad?" And then I paused and said, "Call 911."

I do not even remember what happened. He never called me back, but it taught me that answering your phone can get you work. When someone needs a lawyer immediately, they don't bother with reaching out to someone who isn't available. They just go on to the next one. It also taught me that human beings' lack of common sense knows no bounds.

DISCUSSION QUESTIONS

1. What does "you have to look like a lawyer" mean when it comes to dress and office space?

2. In what ways can you design your office to look both attractive to clients and functional to the lawyers?

2. Every dollar you do not spend on law books or other materials, you put in your pocket. How can you keep up-to-date on all you need to know?

4. What does "I don't want it quick and wrong" mean?

5. Again, what does close proximity to the courts and other lawyers do for a small practice? What are the pros and cons?

6. Discuss the pros and cons of flat fee billing. Does it mean you get to use the fee immediately?

7. What is client 'hand-holding'? Why is it a good practice?

8. What are your thoughts about after-hours client calls? Is it good business practice to be easily reached?

CHAPTER 3

LINCOLN LESSONS: THE PRACTICE OF LAW

LESSON #1:

On Lincoln: *His argument skills far surpassed his legal research skills.* (As do mine).

This is not unusual. Many of the solos I know stop using books and research in year five. This, of course, is a mistake. Graduating law school does not provide you a key to all the legal knowledge. It just opens the gate to the practice of law. Look at the word "practice." Its definition is: *repeated exercise in or performance of an activity or skill so as to acquire or maintain proficiency in it.*

Get the *maintain proficiency* in it? It is not a learn and dump thing, like much of college was, where you would cram and cram and cram and dump everything you'd learned after the exam. I remember the bar exam as that. I spent months preparing for something I barely remember. It was a proficiency exam with little after value. There has not been a case or cocktail party since that I could squeeze most of that stuff into.

This is all beyond the point of Lincoln's being a better advocate than a researcher. This is a plus and a plague for lawyers. In moot court, the student is taught that argument is king. The thing they miss is that the actual court of appeals believes that argument is worth 5-10% of their decision. Ten percent is definitely a nice swing, but little more than that.

The point is that students and lawyers who are gifted in this believe that all they need is a good argument and the win is at hand. Well, not so fast. Research is what matters. Neither of us is Abraham Lincoln, so we better keep researching and then use our advocacy skills.

Never leave a stone unturned because if you do, this could happen:

It was a Friday morning, motion day. In my county seat, motion day is done as a cattle call. This means, basically, first come, first serve. As the drill goes, everyone schedules their own motion for 8:30 a.m. and then waits. Lawyers with several motions travel in and out of courtrooms waiting to find a time when opposing counsel is in the same courtroom at the same time. Once the stars align, they get called. This means that some days you get in and out, and on others, you sit for hours. It is what we do.

A newer attorney on the rolls filed a Motion for Reconsideration with who would probably be called our 'toughest' judge. Tough here means low B.S. tolerance. Basically, a Motion for Reconsideration is filing a motion with the judge hoping she will 'correct her error'. Now, read that again. Ninety-nine percent of the time, it is like filing a motion for the judge to say her kids are ugly. It just ain't gonna happen.

So the young lawyer is arguing about how the judge made an egregious error. This is also something you never do. If you want the judge to rule in your favor, you don't call her an idiot. About halfway through the argument, the judge stopped the lawyer and said:

"Do you have a mentor?"

I immediately stopped reading, as I could sense that the show was about to begin.

"Yes, your honor," the overly confident newbie said. And then she slowly began to realize that she was about to be sliced and diced.

"Did you go over this motion with your mentor?"

"No, your honor," she said, her voice now shaking.

"I want you to take her to lunch. Yes, that is what you should do. Take her to lunch and go through this motion with her. So, withdraw this motion and re-notice it for after you meet with your mentor. She will be able to help you formulate an argument and whether there even is an argument."

"Thank you, your honor."

As the lawyer turned around, the courtroom was packed with lawyers waiting to be called. You could have heard a pin drop. This new lawyer just got schooled big-time by the judge. It was not being run out of town on a rail, but close.

Become better than Lincoln at research, even if you are a moot court star.

LESSON #2:

When you add this to Lincoln's uncanny ability to simplify and abbreviate complex legal cases with his ability to read juries, he was exceptional.

This is the 'kiss me stupid' approach to the practice of law. Sit in court and listen to how lawyers formulate arguments on their feet. They are, by and large, terrible. Remember I said 'on their feet.' This means off the cuff. Well-crafted arguments that you prepare are a whole different animal. The shoot from the hip arguments that lawyers make off-script, although totally necessary at times, are so often meant for a listener who has been schooled in detail over the case.

Take, for example:

> The main point I want to make, your honor, is given the gravity
> of the problems and the failure of the Plaintiff to provide a safe,
> non-neglectful environment for the child vitiates the necessity to
> reexamine the best interest factors and focus on the moral charac-
> ter of the mother with the specific intent of having the factors in
> favor of my client.

Think (and speak): *My client wants custody.*

The way the argument is framed is overly wordy, and it is obvious that it is an attempt to sum up in a paragraph what has briefed in detail.

Everything you wanted to say in longer form should be in your memorandum or brief. But, remember what Mark Twain said: *If I had more time, I would have written a shorter letter.* Remember, what you want to say is: My client wants custody.

I used to work with a lawyer who was a master at crafting, styling, romancing, and strategizing every argument. I would be at his secretary's desk with the latest revision of the brief or letter he was working on, and it would say "edit #23." The first time, I asked his secretary what that meant, she looked at me painfully and said, "that is his 23rd revision." I gasped. It seemed insane to me that he would revise a letter 23 times. She then told me that she had gotten over 100 on some lengthy summary disposition briefs. "Each time, they get shorter and shorter."

"Ah ha," I thought. "This is key: edit, edit, edit." But can you edit to oblivion or until you lose your point?

Take for example, this same lawyer. He was a big-shot litigator and was the head of a large litigation department. Years after I left the firm, I was on a panel of arbitrators deciding a multi-party litigation matter. There were probably 20 defendants, and he represented a minor player. I remember the day I got his brief. I will recite it in its entirety here:

Perhaps there's a reason the Plaintiff never mentioned my client in his brief. **The end.**

This was all he wrote. He was last to turn in his brief, and it was the first one I read to prepare. It was clever and dismissive, and I was dying to see why he was left out of the Plaintiff's brief. It turns out that the reason was that there was no liability for his client, and it was made painfully clear by how the Plaintiff never thought to discuss the Defendant.

This was a product of the 100-edit paper. Later, I talked to him and found out that he had started with a draft of nearly 48 pages. It occurred to him that it was a simple case of no liability. He was dancing all over the place until he got the brief of the Plaintiff. He decided to take a chance and scrap all of his work, which was now only 14 pages from the original 48. It was a stroke of genius that I would not advise any lawyer to do, especially new lawyers, until they are firm in their footing. It could be a costly error. His brilliant move could have easily been an idiot blunder.

Then there was the lawyer who lost a motion for summary disposition. It was a case with multiple deaths, and his client was one of the Defendants, a big corporation. The case was about an individual executive who travelled the globe in the corporate jet, drinking. He got out of the jet, in a tux from a party in Japan just 20 hours ago, no less, intoxicated. He left the airport in his SUV and turned it over in the expressway, ultimately killing two people. The Defendant corporation was sued on a dramshop-type theory. That meant the corporation acted like a bar and served someone who was visibly intoxicated. It was an interesting theory. The lawyer for the big corporation filed a Motion to Dismiss based on dramshop's not extending to a situation or a company like this. He was probably right, but the judge was cautions and remembered the first three things they teach you in judging school: 1) never grant Summary Disposition, 2) never grant Summary Disposition, and 3) never Grant Summary Disposition. This is based on the back theory that every dog should get his day in court. If the judge dismisses out a Defendant, then the Plaintiff will not get it to a jury and will not get the verdict of the people. Being abundantly cautious, the judge denied the motion.

Then the lawyer did something both gutsy and suicidal. He filed a Motion for Reconsideration—but not just any Motion for Reconsideration. He filed a Motion and called the judge everything in the book. It sounded like this

> "If the judge took the time to read the case law, he would quickly realize how wrong his decision was."

To me, it was an astounding piece of brief writing and bordered on the profane and/o r grievable. To think that a member of the bar would write that, and to a judge no less. Wow! I ultimately called him, as he was a friend of mine. "Hey Bill," I said, "trying to get yourself thrown in jail?"

He responded in typical mega-litigator fashion. "I don't give a damn about Judge C. I will probably never practice again in front of him. I am tired of Podunk judges not following the law, especially when it is on all fours.

A few weeks later, we all got an opinion in the mail because in this state, no motion is argued, it is decided on the motion and brief. The opinion said "Motion GRANTED, Defendant Big Corp. DISMISSED."

I just could not believe it. I thought that out of general principle, the judge would lash back at the lawyer, but he did not. That goes to show you.

LESSON #3:

Lincoln: *The leading rule for the lawyer, as for the man of every other calling, is diligence. Leave nothing for to-morrow which can be done to-day.*

Jeff Williams was a senior litigator at the mega firm. He walked, ate, and smoked law. The guy worked and worked and worked. The moment I was paired with him, I knew that it was going to be trouble. It was most likely my undoing at the firm because he was also a perfectionist who believed that no one could do work at his quality level. And he was probably correct. He had very large clients, and he worked so diligently that he would make an appointment with his client the very day he received discovery materials to have a face-to-face meeting on the timing of completing the materials within the prescribed time period allowable under the court rules. He did this not to give favors. In fact, when the 'other side' wanted a time delay on something, he would regular deny the request. A practice that I teach is to always agree to the first adjournment. The practice of law is a stressful career. By being a hard ass, you do not make it any less stressful. You also get a reputation of someone who is hard to get along with. Jeff was not hard to get along with. He was just a time-Nazi. He wanted the litigation train to roll into the station on time and in his favor.

When he would not give any extensions, this would cause the other side to either blow a deadline or file a motion with the court for an extension. If they blew the deadline, then he could file his own motion to compel. This means that he would ask the court to force him to answer or lose some benefit. If the other side filed a motion for an extension, Jeff would reply, "I turned my discovery requests in on time according to the court rules. Your honor, let's all play by the same rules."

This does lead to an odd twist to this lesson. There is a lawyer's karma out there. It is the karma that everyone has in their daily life, but it seems to attach to lawyers quicker because of the sometimes angry aggressive and impatient behavior they exhibit. Several years ago, I was handling, or goal tending, a case for a client who really had no case and just wanted to stall the matter while he figured out what he really needed to do, which was to file bankruptcy. I answered the complaint and received the discovery request. After I answered those, the lawyer on the other side filed a summary disposition motion to basically bounce me out and give a victory to his client. The day I got it, I noticed it was scheduled for a day I was going to be out of town on a long planned vacation. I immediately called him, but I did not receive a call back. After a few days, I sent him a letter asking him to reschedule, and he failed to respond. I finally got ahold of him, and he said, "my client won't let me move the hearing."

Undeterred, I went to the court not to speak to the judge but to see if an appointment could be made for a status conference. When I got there, the judge happened to be in his secretary's office.

"Hello, your honor," I said.

"Gosh, it is nice to see you, you don't seem to get around these parts as much as you use to. I notice you are on a case scheduled in front of me coming up soon."

"That is why I am here. I wanted to schedule a status conference because the other side will not move the hearing, and I am on vacation that day."

"Heck, you don't have to schedule a conference." He looked at his secretary. "Reset that motion for two weeks later."

Then he turned to me. "Is that enough time?"

"Absolutely."

The original motion was scheduled for the next Monday, so any notice of the new date would not reach the other side in time. So I did what any self-respecting lawyer dealing with someone who had gone out of his way to be mean to me would do: I didn't call him to tell him Monday was off and basked in the idea of him traipsing over to argue a motion that had been rescheduled. Karma is a bitch.

LESSON #4:

Lincoln: *Extemporaneous speaking should be practiced and cultivated. It is the lawyer's avenue to the public. However able and faithful he may be in other respects, people are slow to bring him business if he cannot make a speech. And yet there is not a more fatal error to young lawyers than relying too much on speech-making. If any one, upon his rare powers of speaking, shall claim an exemption from the drudgery of the law, his case is a failure in advance.*

Even though I discuss this throughout the book, this cannot be over-emphasized: 90% of the arguments are decided on your writing, and 10% on your verbal advocacy skills. I have taught hundreds of students about advocacy, and dozens in various moot court programs, where they do the verbal equivalent of calculus on their feet during competitions. The moot court experience, which I did while in law school, is unmatched if the emphasis is on the writing first and the oral argument second. Law is filled with hot dogs who think they can solve any problem by talking their way out of it. People say all the time, "I should go to law school because I am good at arguing." This is off base. An argument is something that is carefully crafted, not the first thing that comes to mind as a defense. I used to tell students that I would prepare for 100 things that could happen, and it was always the 101st that occurred. But this was never a problem because I was so over prepared I was ready even for this one. Ideas would immediately come to mind because I had a rich grasp of the facts/law and the blending of the two.

This point dovetails nicely with another of Lincoln's lessons:

Lincoln said about office preparation: "*This course has a triple advantage; it avoids omissions and neglect, saves your labor when once done, performs the labor out of court when you have leisure, rather than in court when you have not.*"

The notion that a poorly researched motion or brief or argument can be somehow resurrected with dazzling oratory is absurd.

LESSON #5

Lincoln: Discourage litigation. Persuade your neighbors to compromise whenever you can. Point out to them how the nominal winner is often a real loser---in fees, expenses, and waste of time. As a peacemaker the lawyer has a superior opportunity of being a good man. There will still be business enough. Never stir up litigation. A worse man can scarcely be found than one who does this. Who can be more nearly a fiend than he who habitually overhauls the register of deeds in search of defects in titles, whereon to stir up strife, and put money in his pocket? A moral tone ought to be infused into the profession which should drive such men out of it.

Let's examine litigation at its smallest level:

I have seen lawsuits that ended up being designed to make lawyers money. I guess you may say that this is at the top of the no s*** list, but until you actually see it unfold, you will not understand it.

Take, for example, Jason Unger. Jason was a guitar player, and he was a good one at that. He made his living as a studio musician and moonlighted playing special occasions, like weddings and other formal-type parties. Once, he was hired by a very busy band to play an entire Christmas season of gigs; there were 35 jobs from November 1 until January 1. In going about a business like this, too many, even those who want to protect themselves, hire a lawyer or even have a contract. Jason did neither. The entire month of October was considered to be practice month, where they were scheduled to practice every weekday evening for four hours to get Jason up to speed.

He was to be paid approximately $1500 per week. This was to start after the money came rolling in. Thus, he was not paid for practice because they had no money stream during this time. This did not really worry Jason as he could do some of his other studio work during the day—but these would definitely stop when they started to travel for the holiday jobs.

The practices seemed to go well, and the band was all ready to perform their holiday extravaganza. On Halloween, just a day before the first job, he got an email from the main man in the band: "Taylor, our old guitar player, has moved back to town and we will not need your services. Thank you and have a nice holiday. It has been nice knowing you."

What next?

This is everyman litigation. This is what people deal with on a daily basis and what lawyers miss because they are too busy looking for the big case. Do you sue? If you are a lawyer, you can. If you are a guy who just got fired after canceling all his own work and has no money, nope. How do you resolve this short of litigation? It is a loss to him of October's practice and November and December work. He has a family and is out the equivalent of three months at $1500 per week, or $18,000.

You know like I am sitting here that the band will say: 1. We did not have a contract; 2. You only practiced with us for four weeks and we never agreed to pay you for that; 3. Even if you can somehow create a contract by your performance with us during October, we never agreed to pay to get you up to speed.

So, what do you do? Does he go to a lawyer and find out that if he gives the lawyer a $10,000 retainer, he will get back, what? If the lawyer charges hourly, how much could it be? Let's say, it is researching law and facts and filing the complaint. That would be maybe $1500, plus a filing fee if you do it right. Then there is a deposition, and since discovery is not allowed without a court order in my state for such a small amount, you really go to trial. You will want a jury, and there is a cost to that. Trial preparation is four hours at $250 per hour. That's $2500, even before the half-day trial, which will cost him another $2500.

So we are now up to $5000. Jason has no contract and played no jobs. He can do alternate work for November and December, but if he does not, he is not mitigating his damages. Wheeeeew....

Get it?

Litigation can be an albatross. You are probably thinking: small claims court, that is the ticket. Well, small claims does not do so well with cases that are not concrete. Just try to tell a client to go to small claims when she breaks up with her boyfriend and he won't let her get her stuff back from the apartment they shared.

Is there a lesson here? There are really two. The first one, to a newer lawyer, is probably not so obvious: a lawyer is not a blunt instrument. You will be in a world of hurt if you always tell everyone you need to sue to resolve an issue. Suing should be the last, not the first resort. The first resort should be finding a way to lower your client's $18,000 expectations by teaching him, through the counseling part of the attorney and counselor at the law plaque at the end of your desk, that he did not actually lose the two months work because, as he will tell you, he found work and made $5000. This means he made 5k instead of 12k, or a loss of 7k. The month of October is not like being trained to do a job and being paid for training. It is a non-contract event, and while you may have a "my time is valuable" argument, it would not be worth $1500 per week. You might have an argument for $2500 for the month, and maybe $2500 in total for the other two months. Remember, he did practice for one month. To a jury, the other months never happened.

So what is the resolution? It is a varied as you are creative. Is it as simple as that your client wants $18,000 and the Defendant wants to pay nothing. Does this mean that right in the middle at $9000 must be the solution? I think not. To every lawyer I know, this is a nuisance case. To Jason, it is Christmas without presents for his children.

Maybe the solution is to do it pro bono for the experience and the undying gratitude of a life-long client. Maybe, just maybe, this is how you begin building a practice.

But do not make this a habit. If you pro-bono it, make sure you know when to cut and run from becoming a legal aid clinic with no pay. There are also lessons on the other end.

DISCUSSION QUESTIONS

1. In the litigation process, when are advocacy skills more important than argument skills? Why?

2. What is the more important skill: researching or argument skills?

3. What was the judge really saying to the 'newer lawyer' when she asked if she had a 'mentor'?

4. The moot court model of argument can become verbal calculus in very complicated cases. Why would you strive to avoid this in all respects, especially in motions and trials? Think of the 'kiss me stupid' approach.

5. Does 'edit #23' seem excessive for a motion or brief? How about for a letter?

6. What does the 'law being on all fours mean'?

7. What does 'everyman litigation' mean?

8. As a solo or small firm lawyer, why can it be good to take practice cases? Why can it be bad?

Too Many Lawyers or too Many Naysayers?

I started practice at a large Midwestern law firm. I was not cut out to be in a large firm, as I spent my life prior to going to law school working on my own. Once you have produced a living from your own two hands, it is hard to go to work for someone. Believe me, working for a 150-plus attorney law firm is truly working for somebody. When I came into the firm, I was one of ten new associates. Ten was a very large number, but across the street at another prestigious firm was another ten who were just hired. The funny thing about my firm was that the ten who were hired were all from other cities and states. There were no locals in the mix. This showed how rapidly the city was growing and how they needed to pick from a bigger pool.

At the time, every name of every partner, associate, and staff attorney was on the letterhead. With there being 150 of us, it almost looked like you needed to start the letter on the second page because all the names covered the first page. I was the first of the ten hired. It was just luck of the draw, but it meant first choice at furniture. It seems meaningless, but we had a vulture system of office furnishing. When an associate washed out, we would be notified according to placement on the letterhead. Certainly, the partners were all well-furnished. Then it was on to junior partners and then associates. I got what I needed in Spartan fashion, but I can tell you by the time new #10 was told he could pick through the office wreckage, only broken pencil sharpeners were left. As a result, you could tell where you were on the letterhead based on furniture. It is an interesting way of doing business, a truly foolish way, but an interesting one nonetheless.

At a firm the size of the one I worked at, client service was left to the partner. If you were an associate, you were rendered nugatory. It was your job to prepare legal research for the partner and say nothing in client meetings; partners only brought you in to view their brilliance and give you a taste of what 60 hours a week could net you after your first heart attack. As a result, you had little or no contact with any clients. And clients were not paying large lawyer bills to talk to a newbie.

I ended up washing out of the firm after three years. It was probably a mutual agreement that I could not deal with many lawyers so full of bull. I remember one fatal meeting with a partner who truly enjoyed beating new associates up. I was older than the other nine and had owned my own business, so my bullshit tolerance was minimal. I had a very pressing issue for my family, and his door was open.

"May I ask you a question," I asked as he sat staring out the corner office window.

"No," he said. "I am too busy to take time for that."

Well, since it was not an option to push him and his $2000 chair right out the 10th floor window to his impending death, I did what a 30-year-old litigator would do—and not what a 25-year-old Michigan grad would do, which is to cower out of the office—instead, I said:

"Next time you need something, I won't have time for it."

Bad move.

I eventually left, but as I was leaving, several partners who 'liked my tenacity' sent me packing with enough of their odd duck clients that I was able to open up my own shop. This brings me to the theme of this chapter: too much competition or the too–many-lawyers syndrome.

First, there aren't too many lawyers. Period. There are, however, too many babies who think that the law degree owes them a career. It does not. This is the entitlement concept. Sure, the law license entitles anyone to practice law. It is hard to get. Not everyone can, and as a result, those who do have a license have proved that they put in time in school. After passing the bar, it is then time to start the real work, the hard work of practicing and developing clients and sculpting your reputation.

What this means is to practice with blinders on. Isn't all of life clouded by the noise in your head that will always try to tell you that you have no chance? Ethan, a former student of mine, always stops me outside the courthouse and says the same thing: "What do I do to get business? Business is awful, and I do not know how long I can make it." On the other hand, Joel, another former student, never mentions it. I see him in court all the time doing this and that and putting little ads in the paper and speaking at a church or community event about something in law people may care about. Guess who is cutting it?

There are the hand-ringers and the 'sky is falling' crowd and, then there is the can-do crowd. You really have to set aside negative thoughts about student loans and what ifs and what should be's. You need to just get in the game, the "dressed-nice, show up for everything law-related" game. You can hide in your office and write woe is me 1000 times on a blank legal pad or you can talk to other lawyers and attend seminars and cocktail parties for new lawyers. Church events are made for this. Everyone wants to know a lawyer, just like they want to be on speaking terms with their family doc. I cannot tell you how many people call me their lawyer. It is a true badge of honor for me.

DISCUSSION QUESTIONS

1. What does 'practice with blinders on' mean?

2. It is obvious that a law degree does not owe you a career. It is, however, a barrier to entry, and that should allow you some advantages in the work force. Explain.

3. What does it mean that there are not too many lawyers, there are too many babies?

4. Why does everyone want to know a lawyer?

5. What is the theory behind not having the associates interact with the firm's clients? Is it because the lawyer is newly licensed or because of the fear of client raiding?

CHAPTER 5

PEERING IN

War stories come with every job, but I would guess the more colorful ones come from lawyers. We talk for a living and get people out of odd jams. It is ripe pickings for storytelling.

One of my clients was gay. He went to a truck stop to try and meet another man. When he got there, the guy told him that he was into bondage and convinced him to try it. The guy got my client into the backseat of the car, removed all of his clothes, and tied him to the backseat door handle. Then he called 911 and split. So there was my client, naked, tied to the door handle, and waiting for the police. How do you work your way through that?

Lawyers make a living peering in. This is especially true of criminal defense attorneys. It goes with the territory. You spend your career dealing with conflict and people in peril. From the lawyer's side of the room, you see the victim, the prosecutor, the judge, the witnesses, and the jury, who will make the ultimate decision. What criminal defense lawyers do is attempt to turn the courtroom into a multi-colored canvas, or a block of clay with an array of textures. They then try to mold it or draw it in a way that benefits the client the most. Benefiting clients the most does not necessarily mean keeping them out of jail. Sometimes, it simply means keeping them out of harm's way, even if it is their own doing.

Every one of those textures or colors could be the seed that provides the Holy Grail of the criminal case for reasonable doubt. If there are enough colors on the canvas, a good defense attorney can say that each one is with a reasonable doubt. Since only one is needed, as the jury instruction preaches, they will prevail or find a way to benefit the client the most.

The lawyer may prevail with his Picasso, but most of his wins are just as rare. The prosecution, also known as the State or the Government, has a similar job, painting on that canvas, but they have odds. The odds are always in the prosecution's favor. The judge will say that the prosecution has the weighty burden of proving 'every element beyond a reasonable doubt.' It sounds intense. It is not. The prosecutor wins at least 90% of the time, and they act at every turn like they are just about to lose.

The defense, on the other hand, wins so rarely that a good defense attorney makes her living not trying cases but mitigating penalties and managing client expectations. A client, who is the canvas or the clay, can also be drawn or molded to accept an outcome created by the defense attorney.

This is the same way that the mind works when something bad happens to you. At first, you are in disbelief. You find yourself in a jail cell. All you remember is going to a bar. Then it flashes in your head that there was a car accident. Then you see and taste blood and panic and do not believe it. If your lawyer tells you that day that you are sunk and to get ready for prison, even though that is true, you would be unable to process it. It is too serious and completely unlike the plan you had for your life. It is the lawyers' job to bring you along slowly from A to Z.

This process may take months or longer. The only thing that is sure is that many times, a good defense attorney can be the government's best friend. It is not as simple as that they want a conviction and you want your client to walk. If it were that simple, then every case would be tried, and our system would be log-jammed. It would not work. The system is based on plea deals, and the job of a defense lawyer is to convince the client of the odds. Defense lawyers work with their clients in an awkward dance to show the clients that they are toast, but also making them believe that your are on their side.

Similarly, defense attorneys can convince the prosecutor that there is a fatal flaw in the prosecutor's case. This is rare because prosecutors authorize a case and would like to think they are all solid gold or they would not have been authorized to begin with. Yet, it happens. Plea negotiation is also a mitigating exercise. Attorneys must politely convince prosecutors that their case sucks or could suck. Needless to say, this is also tough to do. It is like trying to convince someone that his or her child is ugly.

So, what does peering in mean? It doesn't mean you live vicariously through the life of that drunk driver who caused an accident and put someone in the hospital. It really means that you do get to see the darker side of the world where people, either intentionally or unintentionally, find themselves.

DISCUSSION QUESTIONS

1. Why would a client think a defense attorney is 'working with the government' when he or she is friendly to the prosecutor? Is it good or bad to be cordial, or even friendly, to opposing counsel? Why or why not?

2. Lawyers get paid a lot of money to tell people to turn the light switch on in a dark room if they want more light. What does that mean?

3. Why do lawyers have a unique role with people who are in legal peril?

4. Since most every case has a winner and loser, discuss how important it is to manage expectations.

PART II

How To

CHAPTER 6

"Hanging out a Shingle"

Lincoln: *The vagaries of a penny-ante practice.*

To go solo or not to go solo, that is the question.

The answer is clear and discussed throughout this book. Now, forget it until you are able to fly. Flying means that you were well-trained to fall all over yourself to please your mentor.

If that has been the case, and if we can put that aside, it is time for the seemingly gut-wrenching decision to go it alone. This is not simply a financial decision. It is a practice decision first and a financial decision second. Let's face it: you can make a living on your own. Period. The old timers use to tell me that at five years, you can make an OK living. At ten, you will be doing fine, and at 15, you will start to cook. I was older when I started law. I was in my early 30s and would have none of that 5/10/15 stuff. I was shown the door at a mega firm, and I decided it was time to produce and in a big way. I had a baby, and my wife and I wanted more. I had a mortgage payment and a couple of car payments. My wife worked because we needed two incomes, and I came into this business to play hard. I was not going to sit on the sidelines and dabble here and there and do a will or two. I was going to hit it—and hit it big.

The first thing I did was to start working out of my house. Big mistake. I know you may be forced to, but much of your mystique or panache or just plain look is based on your overall appearance. I mean this from soup to nuts, or from dress to office, to the way you talk to clients and the reputation you develop. It is all in the package.

I had already had three years of training, and I was ready to bill the bejesus out of anybody with a traffic ticket. That was the mindset at the big firm, and I was bound and determined to carry that through into my boutique one-man practice. This was also a big mistake—which, luckily, never actually came to bite me in the ass—because before I even thought it through, I checked the local bar and saw that a lawyer was advertising a space for rent. It was on the 11th floor of a 15-story building right down the street from the courthouse. It was $500 a month and included an office, the use of a conference room, and copies. And that was it. I had to get my own insurance, books, furniture, computer, garbage can and, of course—the lawyer's lifeline—a phone. I was renting an empty office, but that was OK. I needed to start this thing on a shoestring.

This is the time in your life when you join the young lawyers' bar and hit your friends up for trading legal service. I was not in my home state of Illinois, where my family owned a few businesses that could have provided me with a starting flow of business. Nonetheless, I had to take the office and hope for the best, knowing that I believed in myself and had the experience of seeing how pretty law was when practiced for a few years. Pretty law was what the big timers at big firms did. They sat in their offices behind big desks with no paper on them. A woman dressed like a movie star (we used to call them *great ladies of the theater* because they worked for the top partners) brought in a piece of paper for the big-shot to review. He or she signed it, and then the paper was whisked away.

The first thing I did was to take the plunge. You cannot do anything or go anyplace until you take the first step. It really is true that the way you eat an elephant is one bite at a time. I agreed to get a phone line and believed I was going to be off to the races. But was that it? Was that all I needed to do?

Starting from scratch was made 100% easier by rooming with two lawyers who had already been practicing that magical 15 years. You know, the 15 where you are supposed to start rolling around in money.

One of them was a street lawyer and always had a drawer full of checks and cases, and the other was a machine divorce lawyer who did divorces like McDonald's does hamburgers. He had an office with a big desk. At the end of the office was a round conference table with a rolling file cabinet that had every divorce form known to man. He sat on a chair with wheels and would usher in his new client, sit him or her down, and go off. By the time his clients left his office, after paying him a hefty retainer, he was ready to clip things together, give it to a legal assistant, and it would be filed the next day. He was the quintessential solo guy who did one thing and one thing alone.

How can you go solo with two other lawyers? Easy, you keep your money and names separate. In my case, instead of doing the traditional A, B and C law firm, it was just me. This way, my expenses were just my rent, like I was in an apartment. I would pay once a month, and the utilities and nonesuch were the other lawyers' job. That simple. And yet keeping it that simple is how you make your living.

STEP 1: KEEP IT SIMPLE

Opening up a practice and hanging out a shingle is not the biggest leap you can imagine. It is not a lemonade stand on the street corner, but it is closer to that than the mega-expense you first believe you will have. At one point in my career, we had an overhead of $100k per lawyer, and there were three partners who did not get paid a dime until all the other lawyers and legal assistants and bookkeepers got paid. We were 10 lawyers strong and had a fancy office. You know, the one overlooking the river with huge offices and fresh flowers. It was baloney. It was a death design as a business model. It was everything you did not need to make a secure career. Who does not get paid when the money is tight? You got it, me and the other two partners. How did we live because we bought into the dream? You got it, off our credit cards.

This creates a tension you do not want to be a part of. It is all based on grinding out the hours, and the focus becomes, yet again, money.

Your family feels the tension, feeds on the tension, and Jimmy's ballgame becomes a text-a-thon or a call from a nervous client that you can bill at a premium because it is after hours. Then you start having billing expectations of the other lawyers and pulling them into your madness.

It becomes a never-ending cycle of hitting on big cases only to be back at zero after you pay off all the firm's credit lines. It is a no go for a career, even though it is somewhat prestigious to have your name on the door as the head partner. But prestige does not pay the bills.

Which leads me to my point: simplicity is the only way to succeed when going solo. Why buy books when you have a local bar association where you can use the library? Why? Because new lawyers have spent three years surrounded by BOOKS. Put that book down. At most, get your state's ICLE (Institute of Continuing Legal Education) books. They have primers that are more how-to books, and they cost only a few hundred dollars at most; plus, they even have a cheaper version online. Your law library at your office will contain your law school books, 'cause you already own them, a few ICLE volumes, and the most recent court rules. These are a must. Own them, love them, and learn them. Carry them with you even though you look like a nerd. The judges will thank you, and no one will laugh you—at least not to your face.

STEP 2: WATCH!

Make a living watching the lawyer you rent from. Make a living hanging out in active courtrooms. Motion day should be your front row seat. Since the courtrooms are open to the public, you will never be told not to be there. The clerk may ask, "May I help you?" The answer to that is "No, thank you. I am just observing."

As I say over and over, I am always amazed that someone will spend seven years in college to obtain the valued law license and then think his or her education is complete. I am not talking about the mandatory continuing education that most states have. I am talking about the trial lawyers who sit in the office and work on cases and then go and try it without ever knowing what the judge likes and dislikes or the clerk who always wants this or that. None of this wins cases alone, but all of it combined wins cases.

One of the first things you will learn is that even if you fake it till you make it, you need to learn to really, actually care about the court personnel. The B.S. artist is seen through instantly. I once had a good friend from a large firm who would never practice locally, as his cases were the biggies out of state. I used to think he would get a case, file an appearance, and then do motions at The Hague. All I knew was that it was way out of my league. We would do mediations in another county in a panel of three lawyers. Two of us were from penny-ante law firms, and we were both well-respected street lawyers. Bill was from a monster-mega-firm-deluxe. It was Christmas time then, and we were serving on the same panel deciding cases in a small county. Most cases were about cows walking through the street and causing drunk drivers to hit a fence post.

The other street lawyer and I wanted to finish so we could travel back to our county and give little presents, like mixed nuts or flowers, to the people who save our lives, the office clerks and staff of the judges. Bill, on the other hand, could not understand this behavior with his big-bang practice. It was our lifeblood, so treating everyone in the court special was a sign of respect. Bill looked at both of us quizzically and said, "My philosophy is *never give anyone anything but always act as if you are just about to.*"

"Wow," I thought. Did the law really make a machine out of him?

This example always makes me happy I hung out the shingle. His corporate law bent was a real kill to humanity. The shingle is the place where the trenches are real, and the lawyer is also the garbage emptier. It is not the pretty law Bill practices where everything is provided. I used to practice at Bill's mega-law firm. When I started there, on Tuesday you could leave your shoes outside the door to your office, and a shoe shiner would pick them up, shine them, and return them afterwards. But it went beyond that. One Friday evening, at cocktails, we met with many new associates from another mega firm. The conversation turned to working on the weekends. I happened to say, "Well, at least even if we work weekends there are donuts in the break rooms." Everyone laughed except an associate from the other firm. He looked as serious as a heart attack and said, "We have donuts every day." 'Nuff said.

STEP 3: JUMP

I will say it over and over: Lawyers stay put because of the benefits, the pay, and the fact that they are scared. Many never consider the fact that they have real value and could develop that value with the money going into their own pocket. My big firm friend used to call it "golden handcuffs."

Hanging out the shingle is a daunting proposition. It takes the kind of person who believes, "I have this license. It says that I am allowed to practice law in this state. The rules are pretty simple, and the law is vast. Go!" It kind of reminds me of Jake and Elwood Blues in the Blues Brothers, "It's 106 miles to Chicago, we got a full tank of gas, half a pack of cigarettes, it's dark... and we're wearing sunglasses. Hit it!"

It isn't a Neverland either. The first clients that you have are basically older, more established lawyers. I call them clients because you will do just about anything to be their bag carrier in order to learn the business. They pass along the history of the legal business by tossing you scraps. Scraps are good. They are teeth-cutting experiences that teach you how to survive. Thriving is another story, but at least you can get through the day.

Next, you advertise to everyone you know that you can do their will or a kid's MIP (minor in possession) or anything else that amounts to little beans. The forces of nature dictate how large a case you get. If you try to play ball outside your pay grade, you learn quickly why it takes years and years to learn how to practice and what cases to take. Yet it somehow seems that you are exempted from those cases by the legal overseer who must have also coined the phrase "God watches over babies and drunks," and, by extension, new lawyers. I use the term 'new lawyers' as opposed to 'young lawyers' because lawyers come in all shapes, sizes, and, especially, ages. Long ago, the practice stopped being college to law school and then into the practice of law at a large silk stockings firm by 25. Naw. The real practice of law is for the warriors of any age who are ready to spend their life with an equal and opposing force on every issue. You must be strong. You must also try to survive conflict burnout. It is the 'everything is another war' mentality.

DISCUSSION QUESTIONS

1. Does 'hanging out a shingle' mean you are going to practice alone? Explain.

2. The terms 'street lawyer' and 'penny-ante lawyer' are used when talking about a solo lawyer who does it all. Discuss the pros and cons of this.

3. What does 'focus on the work, and the money will take care of itself' really mean?

4. Besides getting a mentor, what is the most important thing you can do when you befriend a seasoned lawyer? Discuss this.

5. Discuss and describe conflict burnout.

6. Why are your first clients older established lawyers?

CHAPTER 7

MENTOR

According to Webster's Dictionary, a mentor is defined as follows:
men·tor

noun: **mentor.**

1. an experienced and trusted adviser.

The first thing I can say about this topic is don't practice law without one or two or three. There is nothing more comforting than having a go-to person to answer the dumb questions we all get because, frankly, there are none, but you will be dogged by that feeling in your first few years of practice. Throughout this book, you should be getting the feeling that those already in the profession will act as pathfinders for you. It is the 'we owe it to you' concept. Grander still, we owe it to the profession. You need someone who does not just give the cursory "look it up" that you get at the big firms but someone who takes pleasure and joy in helping you.

When I started my solo practice, I had such a mentor. He not only taught me about the day-to-day practice of law, he walked me over to the court and introduced me to everyone he could, from judges to clerks. He ultimately got me on a prized appointment list for federal criminal cases. This was all due to his taking the time to make me important. He had a busy practice, a family, and hourly cases to do. To other lawyers, he was a bit brash, and he could be pompous, but to me, he was a godsend. I had just left a big practice and would spend an hour on a proof of service. He could open two new cases, draft the pleadings, and argue a motion in that same time.

My mentor was a shoot–from–the–hip sort of guy. The big firm was his belt and suspenders. It was an odd life collision of deciding where your level of service should be and how you can get there and for how much money. I could never be shoot from the hip, but I needed to learn how to be less belt and suspenders because only big companies could handle big law firms. When I was at the big firm, I saw major corporations being billed $100k in a month—and that was just for the preparation of one summary disposition brief. I saw $25k copy bills mailed. Don't get me wrong, they did the work. They made the copies. But they did so in such excruciating fashion that I often wondered why everything had to be a law review project. So much of it was about meetings and learning curve maintenance for the youngin' pups, the brand new lawyers from the blue blood schools who excelled in the rigors of eccentric law and were now ready to define the latest corporate merger on their first day when, truth be told, it was years away.

A brand new lawyer at a large firm has an odd learning curve. She must conform. She must wear the dress code, close her door at night, and leave the light on so she can appear to be there for all the partners to walk by and say, "This is a keeper." You have bosses. They are not your clients, as I have mentioned. They are all the lawyers there before you and the senior legal assistants—and do not ever think that you are above any of the secretaries (as they used to be called). I knew an associate once who went to a legal assistant and told her that he was taking over her office because she had a better window view than he did. When she asked why, he smugly proclaimed, "I'm profit, and you're overhead." Guess how that went over. The managing partners said to him, "We can get boxes of lawyers from the finest schools. As a result, you are imminently replaceable. A superior legal assistant with years of service to the firm, however, is absolutely irreplaceable."

It's all about big, and I was never big. I was the lawyer who wanted to solve problems for clients. I guess I was a small lawyer looking for a living.

Don't let shooting from the hip fool you. In law school, you learn to belt and suspender nearly everything. You research until you are blue, and then you do it again. This is well and good and necessary to get your entrance card into the circus. After that, you will find your niche, and you will have to work with a set of laws for cases that you get better and better at. Then, and only then, can you shoot from the hip—because you have bathed yourself in the finer points of each and every scenario.

There are two types of new un-welcomed lawyers, know-it-alls and gunners. Know-it-alls and gunners will both have a rocky mountain to climb as they both will irritate judges and lawyers alike. A gunner is the person who shoots a hand up in the classroom at every turn to somehow curry favor with the professor. I have news for you: the professors think this is overly aggressive and not thoughtful. Give me the student any day who is plotting and reserved in their manner with a fire in their soul and a passion about their answer, not the hot dog in the front row. Gunners are mostly men. It must be that primal urge to conquer with volume. The subtlety of presentation is lost on many make lawyers. This is doubly true with the whiners. There is no gender differentiation with this one.

Stephen T. Logan was one of Lincoln's partners. According to John J. Duff in A. Lincoln, Prairie Lawyer said, "The intellectual self-discipline acquired through association with the Spartan-like Logan was to stand Lincoln in good stead through many a trying period in the years ahead." He added further, "It is fair to say that no man contributed more toward bringing Lincoln's natural gifts as a lawyer to their fullest fruition." Lincoln understood his debt. Logan "was the best lawyer in the state, if not in the Northwest, and Lincoln well knew it," wrote Henry C. Whitney.

This became playing up to the competition. When you golf with a star, you tend to play better. Add this to the axiom that you are judged by the company you keep, and you know exactly what you need to do. Yet, it is not that simple, and I am not talking just about finding such a character. One thing I have not discussed is that lawyers are characters. They always joke that if they knew math and science, they would be doctors. This is important to know because they are quirky. Many times, they need to be the center of attention. They have an on switch that is always in the on position. They tend to suck the air out of every room. Yet they are vital in this litigious society.

The local bar association can help you with this, but many times, it is people serving on committees just putting in a community service sort of thing. I am not downgrading the lawyers who give time to other lawyers, but I am warning you to be careful of their motives. If you want to be a criminal defense lawyer, make sure you find a criminal defense lawyer to shadow. They probably will not spend much time with you, but as long as you have their ear, that's what counts. This means that you can probably call them anytime you need to and ask how this or that judge does this or that. This advice is invaluable and helps you get your feet on the ground. Getting your feet on the ground takes a long time, I would guess a year to two years. Until that time, you are in a constant state of not knowing how to do the whole thing. You can always file an appearance from day one, but to do the whole thing takes a mentor to take you off the page of the court rules to show you how it is really done.

DISCUSSION QUESTIONS

1. Why is a mentor so important if you are trying to open a solo practice? If you have the training and the license, why would you saddle yourself with a mentor?

2. How long do you need to practice before you can go it alone, if ever?

3. Why must you be careful whom you choose as a mentor? Is it similar to playing golf with a better player, where you tend to play better?

4. What are the two types of lawyers?

5. Discuss doing 'the whole thing.'

6. How would you utilize a mentor? Would you establish a time every week to ask questions, would you meet every month, or would you just call when you need help?

CHAPTER 8

STRANGER IN A STRANGE LAND

"All rise, the court for the 17th Circuit is now is session. The Honorable Robert Benson presiding. All who have business with this court draw near. God save this honorable court and these United States."

With these words, or a close approximation, the show begins. It is a club where the players who are licensed to perform in front of the court are best prepared to get the ear of the judge, who placed so prominently and aptly behind the bench. It is not for the faint of heart. It is best suited for the skilled professional, for several reasons that I will cover after we talk ground rules.

The bench refers to the location in the courtroom where a judge sits. The historical roots of that definition come from how judges formerly sat on long benches (freestanding or against a wall) when presiding over a court. In modern courtrooms, the bench is usually an elevated desk area that allows a judge to view the entire courtroom.

The word 'bench' has a broader application. It also describes the judiciary collectively. The term is also used when all the judges of a certain court sit together to decide a case, as in the phrase "before the full bench" (also called "en banc"). Additionally, the term is used to differentiate judges ("the bench") from attorneys, who are referred to as the "bar." Thence comes the phrase "bench and bar" to describe the whole of the legal community.

It is an odd world filled with Latin phrases and 'good ole boy and girl behavior.' You can feel like an outsider in counties you do not normally practice in, as well as a true insider in courts where you appear regularly. Does either help or hurt your case? It depends. First, you have the 'all ties go to the nice lawyer' theory. Next, you can easily get hometown-ed if you go out of your way to try to big-city the judge. No judge likes to think he or she is Podunk.. You are in their universe when you are in front of them, and those who try to belittle or brush off a judge soon find this to be a huge error.

This odd world also includes lawyers and judges who do this as a staple. Hearings are a daily, and even hourly, occurrence. This just means that the language they use to get through tedious portions can seem complicated and dismissive to clients. Take for example an adjudication hearing in an Abuse and Neglect case:

"Counsel, will you waive the reading of the allegations?"

"Yes, your honor."

"Have you discussed what your client wants to do, admit or deny the petition?"

This means that those allegations he wanted to skip must be admitted or denied. This shows how important it is that you go over everything with every client. It is easy to say you want the allegations read for the record, but it also is a waste of time to the judge and other attorneys in the case. Why? Because you should have gone over them before the hearing.

"The Parents are going to admit the allegations in the petition."

The judge responds to the clients, "Ma'am and sir, is this correct?

Clients: "Yes, your honor."

"This means that your clients waive the reading, admit there is a preponderance of the evidence to support the allegations in the petition, and they understand that their appeal rights are limited because of their voluntary plea to this non-criminal action, correct?"

Huh?

The in pro per litigant who just yesed his way through all this is truly a stranger in a strange land. There is a record being made, a permanent record of you saying, "I understand, and yes." Get it? This is also why you need a specialist who knows this drill.

Let me expand the example:

Both parents are charged criminally with child abuse. Part and parcel with those charges, Children's Protective Services is all over your kitchen. They take your kids because they are classified as being in danger. This is a category one case in my state. Category one is the biggies. So, what do you do with parents who want to plead not guilty to the criminal case and want their kids out of the clutches of the state vis-a-vis Protective Services? They are in a classic Hobson's choice. One the one hand, they cannot say anything to protect themselves from criminal liability. On the other, they can't get their kids back unless they come clean and work on solving the issue that brought the family into the court; this means therapy, psychological reports, parenting skills classes, anger management classes, and so on. This will not happen at all if they simply keep their mouths shut.

Then you have the two burdens of proof. To prove that the parent has been neglectful (here for beating the kids), the burden is a mere preponderance. But to find the parent guilty of child abuse, there must be proof beyond a reasonable doubt. This means, it is probably a piece of cake to find a parent neglectful, with a 50.0000000001 burden of proof, called more than likely than not, for laymen. It is much harder to find proof beyond a reasonable doubt. Add into the mix that the ONLY time a jury is allowed in an abuse case is at a trial on whether the defendant is abusive or neglectful, not at any other of this multi-stage litigation.

So, two fancy criminal lawyers who knew as much as my dog knows about abuse and neglect law decided to file appearances in both cases, the abuse and neglect and the criminal case. Great. It should go smoothly, right? Wrong. The lawyers whipped into action and told their clients not to cooperate with any services at all and not to communicate with any caseworker. This is the Armageddon proposition.

Why, you say? It is as simple as it is complicated. The reason is that even if the clients are found innocent in the criminal case, they are going to lose in the neglect case. The prosecutor may not have been able to prove the criminal case, but he or she sure can in a neglect case with such a low bar. It was like what happened with O.J. Simpson. They found him not guilty of murder, and it was a cakewalk to then find him liable in the second 'civil' trial for wrongful death. This second trial has that lower burden of proof.

What is the upshot? The parents did not cooperate; they lost the criminal trial and then were automatically found neglectful, with the prosecutor just entering the judgment of guilt from the jury and case. The parents' rights were then terminated in a summary proceeding.

All of this was preventable, except for lawyers' trying to simple their way through a specialty. Also, see the chapter on 'Dabbling'.

The skilled professional would have known what to do. People say, "Can I do this myself?" all the time. The answer is, "Sure, you can also take out your own appendix, but I would not suggest it."

I do a radio show on the law and have done it for many years. One of our producers called me one day and said:

"I was going to run over to the court and get the papers to file a divorce. Anything I should know?"

The question was so obnoxious and demeaning and over-simplifying that I was almost speechless. I said, "Not really, unless you have kids or assets or debts or a pension or personal property...."

He responded, "I can just figure that out and get the judge to order the divorce, right?"

"Pretty much," I said. Man, I didn't need seven years of college after all.

"Good luck, man," I said.

Lesson: Never try to teach a pig to sing—it wastes your time and it annoys the pig.

DISCUSSION QUESTIONS

1. What does 'all ties goes to the nice lawyer' mean?

2. What does 'home-towned' mean?

3. Explain what 'in pro per litigant' means. Is this good or bad?

4. Being out of your element is much like dabbling. Why is this bad, especially if you are a street lawyer? Are there specialized areas that are just a bridge too far?

5. What does 'never try to teach a pig to sing—it wastes your time and annoys the pig' mean in this context?

CHAPTER 9

Where Do I Stand?

Lawyers are paid for their common sense and problem-solving skills. But don't worry, you can still be a successful lawyer even if you don't have any common sense. I remember I used to love to make tea. I had this great teapot, and I used it every day during a particularly cold winter. One day, I turned on the stove and noticed water all over the place. The teapot had cracked on the bottom. Pity, I thought. I was too busy to get a new one, so I switched to coffee. It never dawned on me that the microwave two feet above the stove would be the perfect replacement for the teapot. Really! It's pretty sad but completely true.

With that said, I found in the first few years of practice that I did not ask enough questions. Remember, everything is happening for the first time, and everything is new when you start practicing. It is trial and error on a dangerous level because you are potentially gambling with a client's money or freedom. Yet even a brain surgeon has to start somewhere.

My first experience of where I should even stand when I was in court happened in a county several miles away from my office. I had only been practicing for about a year and was really wet behind the ears. I had been assigned a collection matter for a big trucking company my firm represented. We were suing an ex-employee for taking expense money from his company gas card after he was fired. The amount was a few thousand dollars, as the cards were for long-haul truckers who went for weeks across the country and were allowed to get advances for everything from food to bail.

I always made it a habit of getting to court at least a half hour early, especially when I was out of my home base town. The motions started at 8:30, and I was already there about 8:05. There I was, sitting in court in my finest suit, with my well-prepared client waiting to teach his bad ex-employee a lesson. It was not a complicated matter, as the ex-employee had failed to answer the complaint, and now we wanted a judgment against him. I could see two podiums and two counsel tables at the bench. There was a podium right at the bench and another about a few feet back. It was a smaller podium and could hold only one lawyer at a time. Since this was a civil motion, it was fine for my client to sit at the counsel table. We discussed that and had nearly a half hour left.

This is an interesting practice note and break in the story. You have to do witness and client prep, but be careful to tell them to be there two hours early, unless you need every minute. You cannot imagine, until you have done it a few dozen times, how excruciating it is to finish the legal talk and have nothing to say. You already know what you need to about the client, and, let's face it, he or she is not your friend. It is a CUSTOMER. This, of course, means you have to be polite, but that is about all you have. Your client is not a relative either. Conversation with him or her has diminishing returns as the time ticks on. Remember this when you plan two hours for a 15-minute talk.

So the courtroom started to fill, and as it was nearing capacity, I was comfortable in the knowledge that I would be called way down the list, as I was an out-of-towner, and surely the good ole boys would be called first. Being second or twentieth has its advantages. The main one is that you get a good deal of time to see how it is done in this particular courtroom, with this particular judge. One of the biggest pitfalls is being the only lawyer with 'a blue hat.' You want to blend in, not stand in the wrong place or do the wrong thing. It is an honest desire on the part of everyone, especially baby lawyers, not to make asses out of themselves. This is understandable. You learn little, however, unless you bump around the courtroom and are schooled at the hand of an irritated judge. This is more comfortable when it happens in another town—then you can get in your car and drive back to your county, with your judges and your courtrooms.

I knew all was well, as I had my pleadings in order (you find the most mistakes in your pleadings when you are reading them just before you are called to do your motion), and they were perfect. My client and I were well prepared and ready to roll. All I had to do was see a few of these other motions and I would be golden.

"Danther's Trucking vs. Gerry Glen."

"Gulp," I said to myself. They called us first, and I had not a clue where to go and where to stand and how to address the judge and when to start and how long to go!!! Yikes. I was instantly panic-stricken. I stood up and told my client to follow me. As I approached the two podiums and two counsel tables wondering which one I would go to and, I was visibly perspiring. This was me wearing a blue hat. I was the only guy in the room who was clueless as to where we were supposed to go. I guess it was far too complicated to simply ask before the hearing. I could have said something like, "Ma'am" —to the clerk preparing the files for the hearing—"I am not from this county, would you please help me?" Maybe it is because men hate asking for directions or because I did not want to look like the newbie I was. Either reason is just plain stupid.

No, it would have made far too much sense. Probably the most important person in the room, besides the judge, is the judge's clerk. These guys can give you a wealth of information, including what mood the judge is in. I can tell you that on important motions, when I sense that the judge is in a foul mood, I put the motion over for a week. I have done this on more than one occasion because having a judge short-tempered and barking at you is off-putting to your client and can have a lasting effect. A word to the wise: Learn fast that the judge's staff should be treated like gold. They are the gatekeepers to the judge, and they also have opinions that they subtly, or not so subtly convey, to the judge.

I decided to walk all the way up to the podium at the bench, right in front of the judge. I figured if I was going to make an ass out of myself, I should go all the way. So there we both were, my client and I, at the front of the court with dozens of attorneys and litigants.

"What are you doing," the judge said.

"Your honor?" I responded.

"Go back to the podium next to the conference table. This podium is only for swearing police officer warrants."

"I apologize, your honor, I am new to this court."

The cat was out of the bag in a big way. It was not a subtle asking of the clerk silently prior to the hearing. It was a full-blown announcement and admonishment. Not only did my client know I was a newbie, seemingly every lawyer in the county did.

But I learned my lesson. Twenty-five years later, I walk into a new courtroom, introduce myself, give a justified compliment about something with the court, tell the staff I have never been here and please tell me where the judge likes counsel to stand. Pretty complicated?

You end up making a living trying to accommodate the judge and staff so as not to annoy them. Blending in is the motto, and it should be cherished to a fault. You don't want to see days where the lawyer before you gets annihilated. See blood on the streets, and you're next after the judge has a lawyer escorted out by a court officer. "Great," you will scream silently in your head, only to find that if you have prepared flawlessly, using your knowledge of the likes of the judge and staying far away from his or her dislikes, you can turn the judge on a dime. Judges, I have found, do not want to be pissed off all the time.

So you go about the business of not only learning the law but the court and its etiquette. Some judges have a firm policy that you never direct your comments to the opposing counsel. All comments are directed to the judge. This means you should not even look in the direction of opposing counsel. Other judges will kill you if you are chewing gum. And as I mention over and over, leave your phone off. It is inexcusable to interrupt the goings-on with some kind of alarm watch or cell ringtone playing Eminem.

One of the judges in my community hates any form of briefcase on the counsel table, and another believes that winter overcoats should be hung on hangers provided for the litigants outside the courtroom. This is simply about learning the idiosyncrasies of each judge. This goes a long way to you flying under the radar. You should not be at issue in the case. Your client should. Let the judge be who the judge wants to be.

Stand at the counsel table in federal court in front of a certain judge and say "Good morning, judge," and you will receive a tirade of, "Counsel, it is your Honor, and not judge, and you never speak to this court from any location other than the podium." This will you not leave you off your game and will misdirect you from the business at hand if you let it.

A very good friend of mine took the bench after being appointed by the governor. I was standing next to him in his new office just a few days later when another friend came in and said, "Hi Dave." Dave had been his name from birth, and Dave had been the name we used for the few decades we practiced with this nice guy, Dave. Well, Dave was no longer Dave, he was Judge. All he said was, "That's Judge." He did not even say, as I would, "In the courthouse, you'd better call me judge." He said, "That's judge."

I really do not mind at all the special treatment that goes with being a judge. You become the funniest man alive because everyone laughs at your jokes. A marginally funny lawyer becomes a hilarious judge simply because he or she wears the black robe. It is all well and good until it becomes "black robe' disease. This disease afflicts unsuspecting judges who mistake the fact that they have been elected or appointed, not anointed. They are the same lawyers they were yesterday, and when they start believing that magical powers come with the robe, they are in trouble.

There was a judge who learned this the hard way. The president appoints federal judges, and it is a big deal. Part of the drill is that they have to have rigorous background checks for the job. This includes everything. A complete review of their life, especially their life as a lawyer, is made. FBI agents conduct this check, and since it is so extensive, it takes quite a while.

An agent friend of mine tells the story about his investigation of one pompous Chicago state Circuit Court Judge who was now heir apparent to one of the prized Federal District thrones. "Tell him I'm busy and don't have time for this nonsense," my friend could hear from the speaker on the desk of the judge's secretary. All attempts to make contact were rejected. It got so bad that my friend thought the judge must be hiding something and knew he would not pass the background check.

This went on for a few weeks, and my friend ended up having to call his field supervisor, who got directly in touch with the judge and told him that his appointment to the bench would be in jeopardy if he did not cooperate. The next day, the agent got a call from the judge's office with an appointment.

Agent Frensley arrived 15 minutes early and was armed with all he needed to get his work over. He was ushered into the judge's chambers almost one half hour late, and the judge, shall we say, was dismissive. He was rude, sarcastic, and, at times, even cruel. He would say things like, "You couldn't get into law school, I bet. That's why you're only a glorified cop."

Yet, Agent Frensley, who was quite the gentleman and had dealt with jerks before, smiled his way through the interview.

Just as he was finishing up, he said, "Your honor, I need your fingerprints." The judge begrudgingly complied.

After that, he said, "Just one last thing, your honor. Please take your shoes and socks off, as I will need a copy of your footprints for our files."

Angrily, the judge ripped his socks off, stepped in a large pad of semi-permanent ink, and placed his footprint on the large sheets of paper the agent had set out.

"Now are you done?" the judeg barked, wiping ink off of his feet.

"Yes, thank you for your time. I am finished."

When my friend tells this story, he can hardly make it through to the end. He always finishes like this, "And there, framed above my desk, are the footprints of that asshole. Hell, we don't need footprints for a background check."

DISCUSSION QUESTIONS

1. Why does 'where do I stand?' have such a sense of fear attached to it for a new lawyer?

2. Why is one very critical component of building a reputation and lawyering, in general, about learning the idiosyncrasies of each judge?

3. Imagine you have filed a motion in a case in another county. When you get to the courthouse (early), what is the best thing to do?

4. What is 'black robe' disease?

5. Is it just as critical for a judge to earn the respect of the bar? Examine closely the story of Agent Frensley.

CHAPTER 10

[YOUR] TIME FOR SALE

What did I learn at the mega law firm? For one: never to work at another. But I learned a completely irreplaceable skill as well, the skill and art of timekeeping. Billable hours are all that you've got as an attorney. You are selling your time, and you need to learn how to keep track of inventory. There is only so much time in the day, and you need to learn how to gauge actual time vs. cutting time vs. value billing. It is like the old joke about a lawyer who goes to heaven. St. Peter tells him, "According to your billable hours, I thought you were 200."

Too many lawyers get into the very bad and costly habit of forgetting to put time down. I worked with a lawyer once who said that he even bills for 'shower time' when he is thinking about a case. This is great if you are doing a class action suit with IBM as your client. But if you are working with the other 99% of the population, you will need to be judicious. Your job is manifold; you need to resolve a problem. Next, you need to satisfy your client (maybe that is first), make money at it, and do no harm to your reputation and to your client. This is invaluable and takes years to balance. If you are to balance it correctly, you will move forward, and your practice will grow on its own inertia. This is true.

Keeping track of your time not only lets you know if you are profitable, it provides your clients with monthly updates of how their money is being spent, and it also provides a permanent record if you are ever asked to justify your billing. Initially, it is critical as a solo to figure out what you should charge per hour. I can tell you, it is like herding cats to figure this out. It took me many years to discover that you will have several hourly rates. Imagine, for example, that you enjoy representing families in the abuse and neglect system. This is mainly a court-appointed system that is paid on a court-appointed basis. The fees you get paid are much lower than for a retained client. The advantage to taking court-appointed cases are two-fold. First, it is a perfect training ground. Second, it is a source of steady work. I used to say I would rather fill every hour with legal work that pays than wait for a plumb case. I do know lawyers who will not touch a court-appointed case, and, frankly, in my career, I have not done that type of work except for the very profitable or specialized (federal panel appointments). You add to this your experience, additional training in an area, the lack of similar lawyers (or avalanche of lawyers), put it all in a pot, and come out with the 'retained' case number per hour. Of course, you first ask every lawyer you come across what they charge and what they think you should charge. This is the 'duh' that is always ignored. Believe me, they want to help.

If you take cases wherein you are surrounded with seasoned lawyers, what do you do first? YOU KEEP YOUR MOUTH SHUT AS OFTEN AS YOU CAN. These attorneys can smell new blood from a mile away, but they will gladly teach you if you are open and willing. This comes back to the know-it-alls. Newbies who strut around with the constitution in their back pocket will never survive. As a professor, the judges are more candid with me. One judge even told me, "If I get one more newly licensed attorney telling me that the drunk driving laws are unconstitutional, I am going to jump out of the window."

Many years ago, I was in front of a new judge in the federal system. Federal cases are far more complicated than state criminal cases. There is a sentencing manual that is probably close to 800 pages. This means that it is time-consuming and fraught with peril. My client was a guy who was looking at a minimum of ten years in prison. Ten years in a state case is gigantic. In a federal case, it is close to the norm. However, to a penny-ante criminal with state criminal sentences of 60 days under his belt, it is easy to get confused that the federal system is so different. He argued and fought and dealt with me over and over using tricks you would use if you were charged with drunk driving. "We will get a better deal closer to trial," he would say from his state experience. But the truth is that he would get a far worse deal the closer he got to trial. They do not work like the state. Federal prosecutors have a lot of things to do to prepare a trial, and if you get too close, you end up with no deal at all.

We finally got a plea in, and it was the day of sentencing. The defendant must have heard that the judge was new. Being a new judge, however, did not mean he was stupid. This judge, by the way, is the smartest I have ever been in front of. He was just inexperienced. So there we were, and the judge questioned the defendant as follows:

"Have you received, read, and gone through the pre-sentence with your attorney?

The defendant answered, "No, your honor." The "your honor" was a nice touch.

"No to which part?" responded the judge.

"To all parts, sir. My attorney never gave the thing to me and never ever came to see me in the case."

I stood horrified. This was completely untrue and, in some perverse fashion, was designed to create sympathy with the court. It was as though the defendant believed that he would get a lighter sentence or go home if he had super ineffective assistance of counsel.

Without asking me, and without my having said anything, as you never butt in when a judge is talking, the judge said, "This sentencing is adjourned for two weeks." He also told me to bring in support for when I ever went to see him.

To say that I was furious is an understatement. The judge did not know my work or my work ethic, so I guess I understood, but to take the word of an indicted and convicted felon with money laundering and fraud charges in the United States District Court, as well as several fraud felonies in the state court, over mine, hit me hard. I went about the business of gathering an evidence file on the bullshit that the defendant spread all over the courtroom.

So I went back to my timesheets at the office. I keep a detailed record of every case I take on. The jail they keep federal prisoners in my jurisdiction in is over an hour away, so it is no small event to go see a client. The records would look something like this:

Date: January 14; *Client: Jones, Jason- Travel to Federal lock-up, 115 miles, meet with client and review pre-sentence regarding sentencing issues, copy same (55 copies), discuss letters of support and protocol at sentencing.*

Two weeks later, we were back in court for sentencing. I had prepared a memo of every time I had gone to see the client. I had also re-attached the pre-sentence that indicated that the defendant was a 'known game-player with the court system.' As the judge took the bench, I was ready and chomping at the bit. The judge opened the hearing by saying, "I am satisfied that Counsel has satisfied his duties with this defendant." Where he came up with that, I will never know. I had with me a memo that I did not file because I was only asked to bring support. As a result, I just brought all of my records. Then the judge said, "Counsel do you want to be heard on the topic?'

It really was no longer necessary based on his statement, but my ego, small as it is in court, would not allow me to remain silent. I said, "Your honor, my records indicate," and I held them up, "that I went to see my client in federal lock-up a total of 17 times during this matter. This includes the four times I saw him here at the Federal Building."

The judge looked at the defendant and said, "What do you have to say, Mr. Jones? Is this true?"

The defendant said, "Yea, prolly, yer Honer."

"Then why did you say he never came to see you?"

"'Cause he never said anything that could help me."

Now, this was a totally different issue. If he did not like what I had to tell him, or if he did not believe I was helpful, well, that was a different issue than never coming to see him. What he did not like was going to prison for ten years, but there was nothing I could do, except wave a magic wand, to save him. He had sunk his own boat. Your job is to do the best you can, keep records, keep your client informed, and go home to dinner.

Actual vs. cutting time vs. value billing

If you work for a firm, you will be told to account for every second of your time. There are a few reasons for this. First, they want to make gobs of money off you. Second, they—meaning the overlord partners— want to see how productive you are and how long it takes you to file an Appearance. In January, if it takes you two hours to figure out how to file an Appearance because you have been an attorney for five minutes, this may be OK. The learning curve is steep for a new lawyer. If that same Appearance takes you those same two hours six months later or on the very next project, you are either an idiot or a time-scammer, and our overlords do not want either. Maybe they will keep the time scammer, but never the idiot. No one fires an attorney for making them too much money. The problem here is that if you do not get done what needs to be done, your time sheets will make this obvious.

When I first started practicing, at the mega-firm I was at, there used to be a category of time called PDA. PDA stood for partner directed activity, get it? This meant everything from researching a new area of law for the firm to look into to picking up a partner's golf clubs from the repair shop. It was the legal equivalent of a black hole, and although it took time to do, and you had to spend time doing it, it was not counted—except in the hearts and minds of the particular partner(s) you slaved for. It was to be avoided by doing paying work—if you could do it. The associate who turns in big hours is dwarfed by the associate who turns in big billable hours. And that associate is dwarfed by the associate who turns in big billable and collected hours. It is a simple equation, but it takes years to understand, and it is vital to understand it as quickly as possible.

You become a write-off king if you do too many PDA-type projects, and write-offs do nothing to endear you to the powers that be at a firm.

The only way to protect yourself at a larger firm is to align yourself with someone in the power base. This way, you will be able to deflect any of the 'must do' assignments for the partners who are big on getting free time from a ready-to-impress associate. I worked for a guy who had two masters' degrees, a PhD, and a law degree. He used to assign us associates things like fact-checking for his speeches. He was not paid a dime for his speeches. He did it as a feather in his cap at the firm. Institutional advertising of the firm is big if you are at the top. The pre-eminent lawyer who discusses insurance law with a bunch of insurance execs in the hopes of getting their business is a star; advertising is a prerequisite to stardom at a big law firm. I, however, had little or no time for what I believed to be an act bordering on frivolous. I found that busy litigators always have paying projects, and they also protect you with the idea of deadlines.

What you want to be completely involved in is the actual collectable billables. There is nothing like 'em. They feed the firm and your family. This includes gamble cases. Those are Personal Injury cases, or the ones that pay a third on the outcome. These cases are time-gatherers and, possibly, brass ring cases. I once had a partner from a shiny firm in to speak to one of my Transition to Law classes. He was involved with a business litigation matter where he had over a million dollars in billable time banked with no pay-off. Yikes, I thought. I asked him in class, "Does it worry you what the partnership thinks, not bringing in a dime in over a year and a half?" He responded in a "duh" kind of way. "Are you kidding me? It scares me to death. The partnership could make me cut the case at any minute. Partnership meetings now are a series of 'how soons?'"

Yet, when he hits pay dirt, he will be the biggest hero in the firm. This leads me to the perfect firm: the five-member firm. In this scenario, four of the lawyers work on hourly grind-em-out cases. The fifth guy is the big hitter, the guy who aims for the home runs on all the seemingly crazy expensive to prosecute cases: the PI cases, the class action-type case, the wrongful discharge or sexual harassment case that will pay off big. You need the other four to pull the weight of the fifth while he/

she is working on the team's mega case. During the months, or years, that it is being developed, someone has to pay the salary and benefits of the lawyer who is reaching for the stars. This type of case is not for the solo—unless you are living on a trust fund or working out of your garage.

When the case hits or the criminal case settles for a remarkable result, with only a few hours' work, you need to know how to value bill. This means that you, in essence, charge for a result. If you charge a client $2500 for a criminal case as retainer, and you head it off at the pass by resolving it short of their even filing an action, prepare your client for the concept that your quick work or reputation, or both, kept the case from coming together and that they just paid a whole lot of money for an excellent but quick result. The fact that you were involved may have swayed the prosecutor from charging. Then there's that PI case that rang the bell with 50 hours of work and a payday of 10 times already baked into the cake where you get one third but everyone expects you to work for free—until it hits, if it does.

If you are a solo or an attorney who is unaccountable to anyone but God in how you spend your hours, you can take that case on a whim or that pro bono case to help just one person. So, you only have yourself to blame if you overcharge or undercharge. It is all just about time.

Overcharging is a bad idea. Just because your client can afford to pay you a certain fee does not make it right to charge them that much. I had a friend once who once said, "First, you weigh the perspective client's pockets." This means you feel out how much money they have. Questions like "Can your family help you out," are relevant, but beware that you are not in business to fleece people. You are in business to do a good job for a fair price, like Lincoln. Finding out in the middle of the case that you do not have a payment program with your client and it looks like they are going to jail for five years can really put a damper on your psyche. Doing bad work or ignoring the file is simply not the answer at all. You must struggle on and ignore the non-profit status of the file. Judges, by and large, will NOT let you out of a case because you failed to properly protect yourself. You will regularly hear "your bad business practices, are not the court's problem" if you try to withdraw because the client is running out of money.

So, how many hours do you need to work to survive the big firm experience? The answer is plenty. Here is how you need to look at it. You need to work enough to be profitable. Take your salary and benefits and double that amount. This is ground zero. Of course, the first year, you are almost certain not to make a profit. You have to serve all the masters those first few years. This is the time when the partners will monitor your work ethic. Ethic is a euphemism for billable hours. The unspoken quota has always been 1,800 hours per year. At 1,500, you are not yelled at. At 1,800 you are making the grade. At 2,100, you are saluted. Then there is the sad reality that below 1,500, you are suspect, and above 2100, nuts. The powers that be do not like the above-2,100 people because they have no balance, and you need balance to stay in the game for nine innings.

I once worked with a guy who was a 2,500-hour biller at $300-400 per hour, and this was in the 1990s. He was a super-mega partner and never took a minute off. He was a Dictaphone kind of guy and would drop half a dozen tapes on his secretary's desk Monday morning containing all of his weekend work. He never had time for anything—not his wife, kids, health, and friends.

I left the firm and lost track of him. The way the story goes, he had a nervous breakdown at 48. This man was a powerhouse litigator of the highest level. His nervous breakdown turned into him doing landlord tenant work to relearn how to be a lawyer. It was like someone breaking both legs and having to relearn walking. He never did. I heard his nervous system had been stressed to the umpteenth. At 50, he ended up getting early onset Alzheimer's, and at 52, he was dead. Did the intensity of 15 years of slamming through case after case do him in? Did his singular focus on the practice of law above all drown him? We will probably never know, but it could not have helped. And anyway, what a sad life he led. In the end, what did he accomplish?

Discussion Questions

1. Why is billing an art? Is it fair or unfair to bill different clients differently, and sometimes based on outcome?

2. What factors should you use to calculate an hourly rate for your law practice?

3. Name other important reasons beyond financial ones to keep concise billing records.

4. Do you think you can craft a fee agreement that will allow you to withdraw from a case if the client does not make the required payments for legal services under the agreement? If not, why not?

5. What do you think is a fair number of hours to bill per year that allows you to be profitable and still have work-life balance?

CHAPTER 11

TRYING A CASE: PLAYING YOUR GAME, NOT THEIRS

Lincoln: He talked the vocabulary of the people, and the jury understood every point he made and every thought he uttered. He never made display for mere display, but his imagination was simple and pure in the richest gems of true eloquence.

"Lincoln knew that people judged cases as much by their hearts as by their heads. Politically and personally, he believed in the power of reason over emotion. He never liked overt displays of feeling, and he felt that emotions tended to get in the way when men of good will tried to make public policy."

Brian Dirck, Lincoln the Lawyer, pp. 102-103.

This refers to the judge or the jury. You need to make it plain and simple. First, please understand that you will try just a few cases a year unless you are a public defender or a prosecutor. If you are either, the rules are different. You need to play the hand you are dealt. This can be a bitter pill at times.

The process of trying cases and lawyering, in general, is, at times, arduous. You not only have to prepare for trial, to the detriment of all your other cases, you have to focus to the exclusion of all else in your life. Yet, you never know how any witness is actually going to behave and which juror is going to fall asleep. After nearly three decades of trying cases, I often tell other friends and contemporaries, who agree, that we are not old, but we only have a few trials left in us. Throughout the years, you end up feeling worn out, and it becomes clear that a rigorous trial practice is truly a young person's game.

There are ways to get your head into the trial game. The first thing is to understand that trying a long case will destroy your practice. Do not get into federal work unless you understand that you may end up in trial for a month. Just imagine that. The first day, you return every call during lunch. By the end of the first week, you say the hell with it. This is one of those times where a good right hand person, like a legal assistant, is worth his or her weight in gold. With a good legal assistant, your practice will go on without you—for the good or the bad.

With all that said, you have to understand that there are two kinds of people who go to trial: 1. the truly innocent and 2. the true idiot. Trials are a loser's game if you are a defendant. It is about those stats I keep harping on where the state or the government wins 90+ percent of the time. They are daunting odds. The truly innocent are rarely tried because, again, prosecutors have the right to charge who they want. Even if it is that obvious that the suspect is, in fact, innocent, do you really think the prosecutor wants to lose? If you like winning, be a prosecutor. If you can tolerate losing, be a defense attorney. If you want to stay out of jail, don't commit a crime. Easy stuff, but the client makes it oh so complicated.

Take, Eduardo, for example.

Eduardo was an illegal alien who had been deported. The confusion in this area is that if you are here not as a citizen and do not have the appropriate papers, you really only come to the attention of the authorities if you are arrested and convicted of a felony. The government doesn't deport people randomly even when they commit a small misdemeanor crime. As a result, when you get convicted of a deportable offense and are deported, the next crime is illegal reentry, and that is a crime unlike simply being here.

So, Eduardo was in the United States without the appropriate approval. He committed a felony and then got deported. Then he came back and started a family in Michigan. He had two kids, one of whom was a little girl who was born very ill. At the time, he was living with the mother of the child, who was an american citizen. She was employed and had insurance. While Eduardo was tending to the hospital duties of the baby, he was approached by a hospital social worker, who signed him and the baby up for Medicaid. Since the mother had not put the baby on her insurance, it was a God-send that he could get her on Medicaid.

The problem is that he was not entitled to medicaid under the circumstances of this case. He ended up getting indicted for defrauding the government based on his illegal status and the income of the household.

So, what you have here is a panicked parent doing what they believe to be their best for their sick baby.

Here is another example,

Bill was a junior partner at a mega firm. He was a guy who could write a brief like no other, and he produced legal products like a machine. We once went out to a bar after work, and I remember he had four drinks. They were boozy drinks and seemed not to have an effect on him. I was trying to learn to dictate on a dictation device, and he said, "Let's go back to the office (at nearly 8:00), and I will show you how easy it is." So, we went to the office, he pulled out the cases he had already harvested from the library, and turned on his dictating machine. Then I sat there and watched as he dictated a 20-page memorandum in about an hour.

The next day, he had it typed, and he edited it and showed me the 10-15 changes. It was an amazing feat—it would have taken me 40 hours to do something that extensive. The guy was just brilliant with the written word. About a year later, I walked into a courtroom where he was trying a case. I sat there for about an hour while he did his *voir dire* and opening statement. He was, forgive me Bill, awful. He was condescending. He made the jury feel like he was better than they were. He talked down to them and even berated a juror when she could not remember the last novel she read. "You have to remember the last novel you read," he said. It was merciless. It sounded like "You dummy, don't you read?" I could feel the tension in the courtroom.

Let's examine litigation karma:

Years ago, when I was in business for just a few years as a solo, I got a random call from a woman who had not been paid for her daycare work. It was her own business, so she could not get help from the state authorities; she had to figure out a way to collect using the court system. It was for $600, and she had no money for a lawyer. I told her that she should file a small claims action. The small claims court is called the everyman's court; it costs just a few dollars to file a case, and all you have to do is show up. There are no juries, no lawyers, and no appeals. You would think it to be heaven to the judges, but not really. They have to deal without the control a good lawyer has over a screaming and yelling client. Although the courtroom is mostly a place of respect, believe me, lawyers earn their keep by kicking client's shins when they start to go off.

The woman seemed so confused that I told her to get the form, try to fill it out, and then find a way to fax it to me to review and edit. She did all this while I made changes, as well as a list on what to do and what to argue. She followed my direction to a T and won all of her money, including the filing fee. She was ecstatic.

Fast-forward five years.

I get a call from the same woman asking if I remembered her. (You will get this a lot.) I told her I sure did, and she said, tearfully, that her father had been killed in an automobile accident and that he was not the driver. He was the passenger, and certainly not at fault. It was such a sad call, but it felt gratifying to know she called me because I was the guy who had helped her. I was the lawyer who gave her my time and talent to do what I do best: solve others' problems.

I filed suit on behalf of the family and ended up settling the matter for $300,000. The common split for personal injury cases is one-third. I received $100,000 because I was kind to her years earlier. I am not saying I deserved the fee or needed to be paid back for doing what I would have done for free anyway. All I'm saying is that if you focus on helping and doing good work, somehow, things take care of themselves.

DISCUSSION QUESTIONS

1. Why will you only try a "few cases a year" unless you are a public defender or prosecutor'?

2. Does Eduardo show how easily you can get in trouble? Was he acting illegally, unethically or both? His argument would have been that he was helping his client at all costs. What is wrong with that thought process?

3. Why was it a bad idea to ask the juror what the last novel she read was? Note: This is perfectly appropriate in many cases when you have a juror questionnaire that indicates this answer.

4. In a small or solo practice, why do you need to be careful taking cases that may last weeks?

5. As a lawyer, how far should you go in helping people for free? Should you relegate this to pro bono or church work, or should you help people who may never hire you? What are the perils of this?

CHAPTER 12

"I Win All Ties"

This email was sent to me by an Assistant United States Attorney in the Western District of Michigan. I asked the AUSA when the deadline was for acceptance of a plea deal. This is what he said:

"Today, according to the Initial Pretrial Statement. However, we can bend the deadline a little since it's you."

These words signify respect and reflect a career of being known as a straight shooter. What could be more gratifying to a lawyer than to have earned the respect of his peers? We do not get awards for being good lawyers, so emails like this—and believe me there have been many—are as close as it gets to winning the Nobel prize in this career, and I take every one as high praise.

Throughout my career, I have seen lawyers say one thing in the hallway before the motion and then something completely different on the record using the "you must have misunderstood me" shtick. It is obvious B.S., but all you can do is remember the lie. This happens a lot when a deal is worked out in a conference room with another attorney in a divorce case.

"We have a deal?" One says.

"Deal," the other responds.

"It's a zoo in the courtroom, do we need to put this on the record?"

"Naw," says the other attorney.

Naw here means, "I trust you completely."

Okay, wrong.

What is the protocol saying with countries we don't trust, "trust but verify"? You need to be the type of lawyer who protects his or her client. And all it takes is to remember to say, "Hey, let's take a minute and put this on the record," or, "Why don't we write out the whole thing, sign it and have our clients initial it?" This way you will have, as they say over and over in contracts, "a writing."

Family lawyers are the worst when it comes to selective memory. The office phone call about a change in this week's visitation schedule for your client becomes a courtroom battle next week because of what you believe happened on the phone. The solution? Put everything in writing:

May 4

   Dear Lawyer:

As we discussed earlier today (remember your letter is dated), my client wants to have an additional day this weekend for a special party. You indicated that it was okay with your client. Please let me know if this is not accurate.

Yours,

Now, this can become obnoxious. You can paper everything to the point where you treat the opposing counsel as an untrusted member of your own personal bar. Lawyers are busy people. This does not get any less true as the years go by. The lawyer you regularly deal with could slide on this a little, but having things more concrete just keeps both lawyers honest. Then if there is a problem, it won't have anything to do about truth or veracity but about wanting something different, and that requires a court to resolve. What I mean is that your handwritten notes are a given. Something you no longer agree with must be taken to court under the guise of "we did agree to X, but, now, we no longer want to agree to it."

A lawyer I know and respect, and frankly look up to, used to tell me "unless you hate one lawyer a year, you aren't doing your job." What he meant was—and I really do not agree, but I do get his point—you are bound to find problems with personalities, modes of operation and aggressiveness, or lack thereof, among lawyers on the other side. There are simple ways not to hate. First, do not take anything personally. This takes years to conquer, if ever. Next, do not respond to a letter bomb until you calm down.

I find emails and letters that say "if you could control your client better..." Well, reading this makes me want to set the sender's car on fire but I have learned to just take it slow and not respond. You know well that you want to respond that instant with something pithy like "it wasn't my day to watch my client," but, this can only add to the entertainment and anger.

Get used to the plain and simple idea that some lawyers are just fire starters or bomb throwers. They believe that the one who wins is the one who screams the loudest. The problem with that is screaming on paper is useless. I remember a client I had who would write like this to her doctor-ex:

Dear John:

I hope all is going well.
You know our son is allergic to cigarette SMOKE, and it is MY UNDERSTANDING THAT YOUR NEW GIRLFRIEND—WHO IS NOT SUPPOSE TO BE AROUND OUR SON PER COURT ORDER DATED 12/14/14—IS SMOKING IN FRONT OF HIS FACE. SO IF YOU WANT ME TO CALL THE POLICE ON YOUR SORRY ASS, KEEP IT UP. HAVE A NICE DAY.
THE MOTHER OF OUR CHILD.
Mary

So why does "I win all ties" actually work? It works because the judge, the opposing party, the mediator, and so on and so forth have to decide for certain using a sound and credible analysis of the law applied to the facts. There is, however, a factor that no juror or judge will say: It is whether you appear reasoned, well dressed, credible, polite, and aggressive when it is appropriate. This is the package that also gets the tie in your favor.

When I started practice, I did a lot of collection work. In cases like this, if the other side does not show up, which was usually the case, I would automatically win. As with time and tides, you grow up and graduate to the next court up. In Michigan, it is the Circuit Court. This is a court that handles bigger money cases and felony criminal cases. This meant that the case, at that time, must have been a collection case over $25,000 owed.

I filed a motion just like I did in kiddie court and scheduled it for a Friday, our motion day. I got there at 8:30 sharp and watched the judge for the FIRST TIME (which was a big mistake, as you will see). He was a 50-ish balding judge who was obviously big, even sitting. He looked to be 6'4 or 5. He had a booming voice and did not suffer fools lightly. As each case was called, he made quick, decisive, and sometimes brutal decisions. He was articulate and tough.

When my case got called, I walked up to the bench, looked around, and then started my argument without the other side. Well, this was not the way Circuit Court worked in my county. You waited till the other side shows up. Unbeknownst to me, the courtesy extended so far that this could be an hour or two waiting for the other side to show up. Yep, that was how it was done.

I got up there and started my pitch, and then he asked, "Where is the Defendant or Defendant's attorney?"

I basically brushed him off, saying "Not here. As I was saying, your honor..."

At that moment, he looked at the judgment I wanted signed against the defendant for, in essence, not being there, and said, "Motion for entry of judgment DENIED."

I barked back, "Your honor, they are not here."

"I don't care counsel, denied. Next cases," he barked.

I stormed out of the courtroom. Big mistake.

This was all a big mistake for several reasons, most of which had to do with losing my composure.

Now, let's take a look at another example:

Curt was a really good law student. He was on law review and in my moot court class. He was a natural-born competitor. Besides that, he was a career cop who did not want to practice law with his license; he wanted to use it to rise through the ranks as a police officer. He was calm, reasoned, and polite. And he was a natural behind a podium.

When students take moot court as a class, they practice for weeks on a problem and then participate in a competition judged by outside lawyers and judges. During the competition, I often go from courtroom to courtroom to watch my students. At that point in each term, I feel like a proud papa watching his little birds learn to fly.

Now one of the judges asked Curt,

"What if it was your wife who was raped?"

Curt stormed out of the room. Literally, during the competition, he bolted. Big mistake. Needless to say, he lost a competition in which he had advanced to the semifinal round. He also lost the respect of the other students he was against, as well as that of the judges.

What did he do wrong by being incensed by the judge's question, and expressing it so plainly by storming out?

About a week later, I saw him in the hall. I was determined not to say anything about the episode, but he walked up to me and said,

"I screwed up," he said in a limiting and questioning tone.

"Yep," I responded, "but not for the reason you think."

"What do you mean, professor?"

"Curt," I said, "You let 'em get to you. They saw your anger. They will always know how to play you at every turn as a lawyer."

"What do you mean?"

"There is a famous story about the incredible trial lawyer Gerry Spence. The story goes like this. Before trial, he would often do something to rattle the opposing party, like go over, shake his hand, pull him close, and say 'I think you are a son of a bitch.' Then he would smile, and take his seat. The judge was none the wiser that he had just put a burning bag of dog crap on his front porch. It is all about composure and never letting the judge see your temper."

He walked away, hopefully, with an understanding of what I meant. My point may have fallen on deaf ears, or he may have understood that he needs to learn to control himself better or lawyers will know he is a hot head and use it to their advantage.

DISCUSSION QUESTIONS

1. Respect is earned. Many lawyers make a great deal of money playing fast and loose with the law or the facts. Where does that get you as an attorney?

2. Why does 'winning all ties' matter?

3. Why should you make a habit of putting things in writing?

4. Letting them see you sweat can be a bad idea in the long term. Shouldn't you push back and use your temper at times to let opposing counsel know you mean business?

5. Can judges rule against you just because? Aren't they always worried about being reversed?

6. How do you control seemingly out-of-control clients? Clients want to have their day in court and many times, that means they will do great damage to their case. What can you do to prevent this?

CHAPTER 13

NEVER DABBLE

Inconsistent with the jack-of-all-trades street lawyer concept are the areas of the law that truly require specialists or lawyers specifically trained in the nuances of a particular way of practicing. Take for example admiralty law and patent/copyright work. These fields are highly specialized, and the barrier to entry is a special license to practice, so there is no real problem with you dabbling because you simply cannot.

If you are doing your Aunt Hilda's speeding ticket, so be it. Aunt Hilda will not lose millions or be put in jail if you blow some kind of payment timeline. The areas to stay away from are the areas where there is a good 'ole boys (or girls) club surrounding the practice, areas such as workman's comp, child abuse and neglect, felony representation, EPA regulation cases, administrative law at most levels, and federal criminal work, just to name a few.

In the federal system, you can be eaten alive if you are a dabbler. It is no place for amateurs. I have a few examples that should hit the point home and will rightfully scare you.

LAWYER #1: EDUARDO

Eduardo was Hispanic and a recent graduate of an Ivy League law school. By all accounts, he was destined to be a star. He practiced civil law and specialized in immigration. He practiced alone and off the beaten path. He placed his office where he believed his clientele would be, and that was not a bad idea. "Go where the clients are" is the best motto to follow, but also be careful, again, of being out of touch, out of the mainstream, and out of the minds of those who can feed your work, other lawyers.

What was a bad idea was that he skipped the clinic and externship courses in his law school because they were looked at as nothing but play time and a way to kill off the last few hours of law school. Many law schools require a rigorous externship or clinic program, and the students who do so are vastly ahead of recent grads. But others, like Eduardo's peers, equated it to babysitting and thus wrote off the experiential value of having a paid mentor who actually pays attention to the do's and dont's of practice. This is a critical mistake.

One day, Eduardo received a call from a client who believed he was going to be federally indicted. The man knew this because he had admitted to selling drugs to another man who was arrested, and he believed the guy snitched on him. He had friends who knew the alleged snitch, and rumors of him turning turned into reliable facts in the client's mind. He wanted a lawyer inexperienced in criminal law, let alone the big leagues of federal court, to go see the snitch and see if he had indeed snitched.

The only thing he needed to do, Eduardo thought, was to get a bar card to get into the jail, and then he would have a few hundred dollars for his trouble. "What harm could it be to just meet with the guy?" Eduardo lamented to his legal assistant. So off he went to the federal lock up to see the snitch. Once he got there, he sat in the lobby for a while, waiting for other lawyers to come in so he could see how they did this "getting in there thing." He sat for about a half hour, and the day sergeant finally came to the window and asked him, "Can I help you?" He responded, "I have come to see a client."

The sergeant said, "Are you an attorney?" Eduardo responded that he was, and the officer gave him a you-should-know-better-than-that look and said, "Attorney/client hours are 8 am-10 am, 1 pm-3 pm, and 6 pm-9 pm. It's still noon, so you will have to wait an hour."

Eduardo decided to wait, and promptly at 1 came a cadre of attorneys, or at least, what looked like attorneys. They all signed in, slipped their ID to an officer, and then filed out some paperwork about the client, and off they were ushered into the inner sanctum of the jail. Still not feeling surefooted, he walked up to the books they were signing into and saw different books marked: Clergy, Professionals, and Attorneys.

He looked at the sign-in sheet and saw that no one was paying attention to the paper clip-barded sheet. Since he saw that everyone who left did not even look at the sheet, let alone sign out, he decided to skip it. He knew the inmate was represented, so this would avoid any trouble with his lawyer. Let's face it, who would believe an inmate over a licensed attorney?

He gave his law license (bar card), as well as his driver's license, to the duty officer, who kept them and exchanged them for a green clip on badge that said "LAWYER." As he entered the jail with the nametag in his pocket, he eyed his page of notes designed to question the snitch as to whether he had thrown his paying client under the bus.

When he reached cellblock C1, the guard in the glass tower barked #109. He was confused, but when he looked around, he saw that there were a few dozen tiny rooms with half-glass doors with numbers on each. He saw #109 and felt empowered because he did not have to ask anyone about what to do. As he walked into the conference room, a sick feeling came over him. Once he opened the door, a light came on. The room was cinder block and was no bigger than 6' x 6'. He had closets in his house bigger than this. Claustrophobia began to set in. The only things that were there was a table and two chairs. There weren't even any outlets or bookshelves, just the plastic chairs.

He sat there for what seemed to be an hour, waiting for the snitch. Every few minutes, he got up to make sure the door to the courtyard where the glass tower was would still open. It did.

He soon heard the guard in the tower turn on a microphone and say "109." This must have been direction to the prisoner. The door to his tiny conference cell opened, and a Hispanic man in his 40s reached out his hand to tell him his name. He introduced himself as Enrico.

"How do you do, Enrico? I am a friend or an acquaintance of yours, Stan. He told me to tell you that your wife and kids are fine and your son is on a new soccer team." Once these words were spoken, his fate was sealed. Yet the young lawyer could not leave it at that.

When the FBI contacted him about witness tampering, he lied. You cannot lie to a federal agent.

18 U.S. CODE § 1001 - STATEMENTS OR ENTRIES GENERALLY

(a) Except as otherwise provided in this section, whoever, in any matter within the jurisdiction of the executive, legislative, or judicial branch of the Government of the United States, knowingly and willfully—

> (1) falsifies, conceals, or covers up by any trick, scheme, or device a material fact;
>
> (2) makes any materially false, fictitious, or fraudulent statement or representation; or
>
> (3) makes or uses any false writing or document knowing the same to contain any materially false, fictitious, or fraudulent statement or entry;
>
> shall be fined under this title, imprisoned not more than 5 years or, if the offense involves international or domestic terrorism (as defined in section 2331), imprisoned not more than 8 years, or both. If the matter relates to an offense under chapter 109A, 109B, 110, or 117, or section 1591, then the term of imprisonment imposed under this section shall be not more than 8 years.

(b) Subsection (a) does not apply to a party to a judicial proceeding, or that party's counsel, for statements, representations, writings or documents submitted by such party or counsel to a judge or magistrate in that proceeding.

(c) With respect to any matter within the jurisdiction of the legislative branch, subsection (a) shall apply only to—

(1) administrative matters, including a claim for payment, a matter related to the procurement of property or services, personnel or employment practices, or support services, or a document required by law, rule, or regulation to be submitted to the Congress or any office or officer within the legislative branch; or

(2) any investigation or review, conducted pursuant to the authority of any committee, subcommittee, commission or office of the Congress, consistent with applicable rules of the House or Senate.

As a complete aside, watch this with federal cases. The case in chief may be fraud of some kind, and when this happens, you never hear the fraud charges brought to fruition because they charge for lying to a grand jury instead. The Feds have resources that are vast. They can slice and dice any transcript made against anything ever said to a federal agent. If they want you, they get you.

Back to the story: So, not only did Eduardo tell the agent that he did not threaten Enrico, he had failed to sign in at the jail—which he thought gave him a cloud of anonymity—and told the agent that he had not even been there. I mean, he probably thought even if his client was to get indicted, they would never be in the same trial together again, so there was no threat of putting two and two together.

There are so many ethical and legal and criminal things wrong with this scenario, that all I can figure is that he believed he was either acting as a private investigator or was being stealthy and winning at all costs for his few hundred-in-fees client. Needless to say, he was indicted for lying to a federal agent and witness tampering and witness intimidation. Why witness intimidation? Well, apparently, a certain drug gang uses threats like "your wife and children are fine..." to tell the man inside they know where his family is and he better keep his mouth shut. Well, he didn't know that, but ignorance of the law is no excuse, and you get my drift.

Sadly, Eduardo lost his license to practice, which is what happens when you are convicted of a felony. He lost his little house/office on a main street that he had bought with a loan to start up his practice. He went to prison. But most importantly, he lost his reputation. And what was tragic was that it was more a case of ignorance than larceny in his soul. It was a complete misunderstanding of how the law works and him trying to play at the razor's edge of the law.

LAWYER #2: EMMA

A far more subtle career destroyer is exemplified in the case of Emma Chambers. She was a newly-licensed lawyer, and she was dating a lawyer who was one of the go-to guys for criminal law. He could not get her on any court-appointed lists, as she hadn't practiced long enough yet, but he could give her his overflow of clients. Many times, a client walks into your office with a friend who has also been arrested on the same case. This happened to him all the time, and he was always ready to pass around the good fortune.

On this occasion, he was representing the target in a multi-defendant criminal case. He was also approached by a little player in the case with a request to represent him. He thought it was just the perfect case for Emma because he could do the heavy lifting, and she could learn from him at the end of the counsel table. It was a "no harm no foul" case where she mostly could listen and learn.

The trial started, and the parties entered into a stipulation to sequester the witnesses. The witnesses were all instructed to leave the courtroom, and the jury was brought in for day #1. The trial started smoothly, and when the judge got around to Emma for cross examination, she did what her boyfriend told her to do, "No questions, your honor."

This was a safe and harmless way to go. The first "do no harm" motto is the most important thing with a criminal client. They are already in enough trouble most of the time, so do not dig the hole deeper.

At the morning break on day #2, Emma thought she would try to help the cause of both clients, and while her boyfriend was outside smoking, she went up to one of the sequestered witnesses and started discussing the testimony that was going on in the trial. She thought that the witness should be aware that the person testifying was saying something different than they all thought—valuable information for sure but unethical as all hell. The witnesses were all sequestered. This means that they are NOT to know what is going on with the testimony BY COURT ORDER. A prosecutor witnessed her just sitting in front of the courtroom, not even out of sight, like she was in her right mind. It was a mistake of innocence or naiveté, but it was a critical error. It was malpractice, unethical lawyering, and witness tampering all in one. It was a whole box of wrong and a career killer.

When her behavior was brought to the judge's attention, the prosecutor asked for a mistrial. The party Emma was talking to was a minor witness, but a witness nonetheless. Emma ended up getting a reprimand from the state Grievance Commission and was suspended from practicing law for 180 days, with an admonition from the judge that he no longer would find her welcome in his court.

DISCUSSION QUESTIONS

1. Discuss the difference between dabbling and street-lawyering. Is there any difference between? Would you call it dabbling if you did your first will for your great-aunt Sara?

2. What is the big deal about Federal Court? Isn't it just state court work in a bigger building?

3. You have a law license, shouldn't you be able to do any law and charge for it (absent special license work)?

4. How do you break into Federal work, or even State Felony work? If you should never dabble, how do you ever get to practice in complex areas?

5. Discuss what the new lawyer did wrong by talking with sequestered witnesses in the hallway.

CHAPTER 14

How Can You Represent Those People?

Here's a Facebook post of mine from 2015:

Yesterday, as I celebrated a dismissal of all felony charges obtained for my client, I was asked..... "How can you represent "those" people?" I can bet that all criminal defense lawyers are asked this.... "the question." Defense lawyers try to find the humanity in the people we represent, no matter what they may have done; after all, none of us would want to be defined by the very worst thing we ever did.

And after all, one day, for whatever reason, you may ended up being one of "those" people accused of a crime.

As New York criminal defense attorney Don Murray so nicely once said, "someday, God forbid, YOU may be arrested. And when the whole world "knows" you are guilty even if you aren't; when the vast and virtually limitless resources of the Government are arrayed against you to ruin your life and take your freedom, there will be at least one person on this earth who will agree to stand up and fight for YOU against those fearsome odds – a criminal defense attorney. Even as you scorn defense attorneys, one of us will take up your cause and single handedly, if need be, take an opponent (the government) who has more lawyers, more experts, and more money than you can even imagine. As they seek to drag you through the very gates of Hell, a defense attorney will be there to stand against them all - your last and best hope.

Being a criminal defense lawyer is a job that our Founding Fathers believed to be so important to a free society that they wrote it into our Constitution. Take a look at the United States Constitution. Check where it says, "Sixth Amendment". If you read the Sixth Amendment, you will find a part that says, "...and to have the assistance of counsel for his defense". That's a criminal defense attorney. That's our job. That's a criminal defense lawyer written right there into the blueprint for our society.

When the vast and virtually unlimited resources of the Government are arrayed against a person accused of a crime, a defense lawyer is guaranteed a chance to stand up for the accused. No matter what. It is a fundamental principle of our freedom. The honor of my job seemed to be self-evident to our Founding Fathers. How strange it is not so self-evident to many of the people who enjoy the freedom they created today.

As criminal defense attorneys, we are honored to follow in the footsteps of some of this country's greatest heroes. And I don't mean hero in the modern watered down sense of the term. I mean real heroes. People like John Adams and Abraham Lincoln (to name only two) were criminal defense lawyers at one time in their lives. In fact, John Adams declared toward the end of his life that one of his greatest services to our country was successfully to defend the British Soldiers.

For my own part, I know that at the end of my career I will be able to "strip my sleeves and show my scars" won in the battlefields of freedom in which I fight. I will look back and remember courtroom battles where the stakes were not piles of money, but human freedom. I will remember glorious life altering victories and heart-wrenching defeat.

And like John Adams, I will know that I served my country well.

A Criminal Defense Attorney

I have maintained throughout my career that litigation is litigation is litigation. When I worked as an associate for a big firm, there were so many litigators that I used to call it the China department. There were probably four litigators to every business lawyer. The rap was that we would fix in court whatever the business lawyers screwed up on paper.

I worked with lawyers who were doing roofing litigation for one case and contract dispute over royalties in another. At some level trial work is trial work, and a trial lawyer uses the same skills, just like a plumber can fix toilets and showers and sewer lines, which are all plumbing-related. This is universally true—until you come to criminal law. It is not just a specialty, it is a calling, if you will. You must become a "vigorous defender of lost causes" if you want to become a good defense lawyer. The rules of lawyering are all different if you mount the criminal business, even from the side of the prosecutor.

I once had a Federal Prosecutor seek me out to tell me "You have a remarkable ability to communicate." I was truly flattered. He continued, "You can translate the case from Defendant to Prosecutor and make both parties feel you are talking their language. The defendant has what we believe to be a ridiculous defense, and the prosecutor has an unbending position, and you can filter these two opposite poles into a cohesive position that somehow seems to make sense to both." Whoa! That was probably the best compliment I have ever had. It takes so much on so many levels to look at the criminal business this way, anyway. First, you are a translator. It is obvious to the prosecutor that the Defendant did it. They drank the Kool-Aid, and they are not going back unless they lose at trial. The underlying proposition is they would not have charged the Defendant if they had thought she was innocent. They have this little concept called "beyond a reasonable doubt" to deal with, and because of this, they are very careful to keep their win record to near 100%.

Then you have your client, who for whatever reason, many times believes that miracles occur and that God will not allow him to go to prison. The former is true; the latter, maybe. God, as one judge so aptly put it, may have many things for you to do in prison to further his word. With a backdrop like this on, say, 95% of your cases, you will have to learn how to dance in front of not only your client and prosecutor but also the judge, the jury, and the presentence department, after you most likely lose.

The odds of winning a state criminal case are about 5%; for a federal case, it is about 3%; and for any appeal, less than 2%. There you go. It is seemingly a hopeless business. Prosecutors only indict where they can win. This leads to the conundrum of the "meet'em and plead 'em" approach to representation. With the odds so staggeringly out of whack, it almost seems silly to do anything but to plead guilty and move on to the next case.

Let me show you something: A client was arrested for a road rage incident. He was weaving in and out of traffic and harassing the driver in front of him. When the other driver forced him off the street and into the shoulder, he pulled up next to him and threw a metal thermos at his car, caused several hundred dollars in damages. He was charged with Reckless Driving, a misdemeanor with a hefty license suspension; Malicious Destruction of Property (MDOP), around $200-$1000 worth, a serious misdemeanor (a one year as opposed to the normal 93 day misdemeanor); and Leaving the Scene of Property damage Accident, another misdemeanor.

This is no-biggie of a case, and one where there is little chance of jail. The reason I knew this was because I knew the court, the way the judges operate, and the background of the client. He had a clean record and was a 35-year-old father of two, with a good job. So what do you do here?

The way the system works where I practice on misdemeanor cases is that a client is arrested, booked, and maybe lodged overnight. After he is let out (usually drunk driving is overnight, but not this) he will be arraigned, a bond will be set, and a pre-trial will be scheduled. The pretrial is the time and place where the defense attorney gets her first crack at talking to a prosecutor usually one on one. Prior to the 'meeting,' you will be provided with a police report, and you will have to interview your client in your office. The first thing you MUST learn is that "there are three sides to every story, the prosecutors, the defendant's, and the one that probably happened."

They will most likely schedule ten or fifteen minutes per case, and it is usually "here is the offer." Please remember that you should not spend any reputation capital trying to convince the prosecutor that he or she screwed up by arresting your client. The real analysis here is how to get to a place where, even if you two disagree, you can get to a place where you can say, "Thank God we have a jury to decide." Get it? They are not in the business of dumping cases because you have a better story.

On this particular case, I had a newbie law student prosecutor. Such attorneys have marching orders, and they cannot budge from those, even though this prosecutor happened to be a student of mine. I got a lot of respect, but no rhythm on the case. The way this works is a senior attorney at the Prosecutor's office writes an offer, and the extern basically reads it to me.

"Sorry, Professor (nice touch in front of my client), we will offer a no-jail recommendation, but this was a road rage incident, and we have an 'office policy' against further negotiation."

"O.K., please schedule me for the second pre-trial. Have a nice day."

Now, do you sit around and argue with someone whose hands are tied? Naw. That would be a waste of time. Meanwhile, the client is both hot because he said that the other party caused the incident, and he's scared because he better plead to avoid jail.

The police report on the case said, "We interviewed the Defendant, and he said that the other driver caused the incident and that he did not thrown anything at the car."

There are two problems with this: Don't lie to a cop. This is especially true when page 2 of the report is from a driver driving by who also called 911 and said, "then he threw..." Second, don't leave the scene of the crime. This just makes you look guilty from jump because the person who calls in the crime usually wins. This is especially true with the spouse who calls 911 during a fight, but many times the caller is gaming the system. He or she just wants to get the cops over to the house to give a platform to embarrass or teach the partner a lesson. Later, if he says, "I didn't do anything," it is usually met with a resounding, "Sure you didn't."

Next chapter was pre-trial number 2. This time, it was with a full-time prosecutor who was an old friend. Being old friends, by the way, does not mean you will get gifts. But it does go back to my "I win all ties" theory because I have spent a career not burning bridges.

This pre-trial was out of earshot of any Defendant, which, many times, is the way to go. Law is just like making sausage, it is not pretty.

"What do 'ya got for me?" I said.

"OK we can reduce the Reckless to Careless and dump the Leaving the Scene."

The translation to this was that the driving offense was now a ticket, and the other was gone. So, he was left with a ticket and a serious misdemeanor.

"No jail rec still in place?"

"Sure," said the prosecutor.

This is not an example of masterful lawyering skills; neither does it mean that you can work down the prosecutor (it is the opposite in the federal system in my experience. The closer to trial, the worse the deal), it is an example of keeping your eye on the ball just for this client when the prosecutor is dealing with dozens a day. You are the private advocate for a less sucky resolution. It was getting less sucky.

In my jurisdiction, the next step is a final pre-trial, and then on to a jury pick and then trial. The final pretrial is usually with the judge and prosecutor. On this one, the judge basically said, "Are you accepting the offer?"

My response was that we would if we could reduce the MDOP to a Creating a Disturbance, a small misdemeanor.

The judge then looked at the prosecutor, who said, "I will have to call the victim, but I will reduce the MDOP to under $200 as long as he pays restitution on the damage." We left it at that.

A few weeks later, I waived the jury, so I did not have to show up for that. I did this because the worst thing we were going to get was no jail and a smaller MDOP. We were never going to try it, but the prosecutor did not know that.

A week before the trial, another prosecutor, a clean-up person, called me and asked "We trying this?"

I said, "Give me a Creating a Disturbance (disorderly conduct) and he will plead."

"Schedule the plea before trial and you got it."

There was no mention of calling the victim or anything other than on this one; I wore them out. It took about three months, and the client became really antsy, but the end result was that one count was dismissed, reducing the other two, one of which became a ticket (a civil infraction) with no driver's license suspension.

This was all a result of keeping an eye on the ball and as a result a good result of a case where the client swears he was not the aggressor. Since he lied to the cop, he could not take the stand—I could not let him, so he knew he had to plead. Some lawyers will plead at the first chance to get the most of the money they got, but that is looking out for themselves instead of their clients.

"Those people" are just people. We make mistakes, and we need master mitigation experts managing their way through the court system. There is a great value in having a tour guide. That would look nice on a shingle: *lawyer and court system tour guide.*

Here's something I'd like to share.

NOTES FROM AN OVERWORKED PUBLIC DEFENDER

First, let me say I love my job and it is a privilege to work for my clients. I wish I could do more for them. That being said, there are a few things that need to be discussed.

You have the right to remain silent. So SHUT THE F... UP. Those cops are completely serious when they say your statements can and will be used against you. There's just no need to babble on like it's a drink and dial session. They are just pretending to like you and be interested in you.

When you come to court, consider your dress. If you're charged with a DUI, don't wear a Budweiser shirt. If you have some miscellaneous drug charge, think twice about clothing with a marijuana leaf on it or a t-shirt with the "UniBonger" on it. Long sleeves are very nice for covering tattoos and track marks. Try not to be visibly drunk when you show up.

Consider bathing and brushing your teeth. This is just as a courtesy to me who has to stand by you in court. Smoking five generic cigarettes to cover up your bad breath is not the same as brushing. Try not to cough and spit on me while you speak and further transmit your strep, flu, and hepatitis A through Z.

I'm a lawyer, not your fairy godmother. I probably won't find a loophole or technicality for you, so don't be pissed off. I didn't beat up your girlfriend, steal that car, rob that liquor store, sell that crystal meth, or rape that 13 year old. By the time we meet, much of your fate has been sealed, so don't be too surprised by your limited options and that I'm the one telling you about them.

Don't think you'll improve my interest in your case by yelling at me, telling me I'm not doing anything for you, calling me a public pretender, or complaining to my supervisor. This does not inspire me; it makes me hate you and want to work with you even less.

It does not help if you leave me nine messages in 17 minutes. Especially if you leave them all on Saturday night and early Sunday morning. This just makes me want to stab you in the eye when we finally meet.

For the guys: Don't think I'm amused when you flirt or offer to "do me." You can't successfully rob a convenience store, forge a signature, pawn stolen merchandise, get through a day without drinking, control your temper, or talk your way out of a routine traffic stop. I figure your performance in other areas is just as spectacular, and the thought of your shriveled unwashed body near me makes me want to kill you and then myself.

For the girls: I know your life is rougher than mine and you have no resources. I'm not going to insult you by suggesting you leave your abusive pimp/boyfriend, that you stop taking meth, or that your stop stealing shit. I do wish you'd stop beating the crap out of your kids and leaving your needles out for them to play with because you aren't allowing them to have a life that is any better than yours.

For the morons: Your second grade teacher was right—neatness counts. Just clean up! When you rob the store, don't leave your wallet. When you drive into the front of the bank, don't leave the front license plate. When you rape/assault/rob a woman on the street, don't leave behind your cell phone. After you abuse your girlfriend, don't leave a note saying that you're sorry.

If you are being chased by the cops and you have dope in your pocket—dump it. These cops are not geniuses. They are out of shape and want to go to Krispy Kreme and, most of all, go home. They will not scour the woods or the streets for your two grams of meth. But they will check your pockets, idiot. Two grams is not worth six months of jail.

Don't be offended and say you were harassed because the security was following you all over the store. Girl, you were wearing an electronic ankle bracelet with your mini skirt. And you were stealing. That's not harassment, that's good store security.

And those kids you churn out: how is it possible? You're out there breeding like feral cats. What exactly is the attraction of having sex with other meth addicts? You are lacking in the most basic aspects of hygiene, deathly pale, greasy, grey-toothed, twitchy, and covered with open sores. How can you be having sex? You make my baby-whoring crackhead clients look positively radiant by comparison.

"All the money is gone now." Not a defense.

"The b..... deserved it." Not a defense.

"But that dope was so stepped on, I barely got high." Not a defense.

"She didn't look thirteen." Possibly a defense; it depends.

"She didn't look six." Never a defense, you just need to die.

For those rare clients who say thank you, leave a voice mail, send a card, or flowers, you are very welcome. I keep them all, and they keep me going more than my pitiful COLA increase.

For the idiots who ask me how I sleep at night, I sleep just fine, thank you. There's nothing wrong with any of my clients that could not have been fixed with money or the presence of at least one caring adult in their lives. But that window has closed, and that loss diminishes us all.

Author Unknown

Pretty true.

DISCUSSION QUESTIONS

1. Isn't litigation just litigation, whether it is roofing litigation or criminal litigation?

2. How do you actually manage expectations?

3. Discuss why celebrity trials with fabulous results do not help the practice of law and the perception of outcomes?

4. Why is a lawyer's greatest asset the ability to keep an eye on the ball?

5. Discuss "Notes from an Overworked Public Defender."

CHAPTER 15

The Odds: The Only Math Lawyers Need

When my youngest child was born, he was two pounds, three months early, and had a tumor on his aorta. Yep, it seemed pretty dismal. Besides being a well-adjusted and healthy adult now, the experience taught me several things about being a lawyer. He was in the hospital for nearly two years for his 23 operations. The experience teaches you about humanity, happiness in small victories, and delayed sadness through the mind games you learn to play called diversion.

Being in the medical world for an extended period of time, especially with a lawyer's training, is a unique and daunting experience. You are trained and well paid to analyze everything. You can solve nearly any worldly problem based on research and hard work. This is not the case in medicine for the layman. My knowledge of medicine is zero. I used to say, "My dog knows more about medicine than I do." This, however, does not stop the raging mind from calculating and attempting to solve the problem at hand. It is a whirling dervish of thoughts, especially when a family member is so vulnerable is in peril.

I remember one night, at about midnight, I was standing at his incubator, and one of the doctors came by and looked at some test results. He looked up at me and said that my son had a grade 2 brain bleed. I asked him what that meant, and he said something akin to "There are three grades. Grade 1 one is retardation as a result, and grade 3 is no big deal." It could have been the other way around, but you get the idea. Then he started to walk away, saying, "Have a good night." "Have a good night?" I thought. I was outraged at what I perceived to be his ho-hum attitude on my son's condition. I had taken a very low profile until this night because I knew that the word LAWYER was written all over the file.

"Doctor," I blurted. He turned around, and I continued, "You, in effect, have just told me that my son has a 50/50 chance of being retarded, and you call it a good night and walk away." He responded that it was not that simple and began spouting off the "'Ya never know," kind of crap. So I pressed as a trial lawyer would when threatened. "Well," I said, "That just is not going to work. Let me explain from my perspective. When I am representing, say, someone charged with a criminal offense. I know who my client is, what he is charged with, and the seriousness of the offense. Then I know who the judge is, the prosecutor assigned to the case, and the possible defenses or lack thereof. If I add the time of year, the courtroom and its comfort, the projected length of the trial, the evidentiary objections, the motions in limine, the discovery, and the jurors who are assembled and ultimately picked, I can then make a very educated guess, if you will, as to the percentage of the outcome. I can look the client in the eye and say, based on all the above, plus the fact that the prosecutor wins 90% of the time, you have x odds of prevailing."

His response was not the point, and the bleed happened to turn out fine. In the end, I learned that we are just people, nothing more and nothing less. The professionals are just that. They are there to guide us in our confusion and through the fear. One of the nurses told me once that my file really did have the word LAWYER written on it. They had a meeting on how to handle me and my questions, and one of the nurses said, "I know how to handle him, treat him like a dad: A very scared dad." Amen, I said to that!

So, spilling that over to its application here, you are, in essence, the logical parent of your clients in this time of peril. You are the expert, the professional, and the tour guide. Give them their odds. Tell them it is not just a guess but also a reasoned and well-thought conclusion.

Everyone knows you cannot predict the future and what the judge will do, yet you should always add that you can never know.

Take, for example, a friend of mine was a try-everything lawyer named John. John was a winner. He was the kind of guy who would try a case because of the old truism that you never know what people would do. He is the sort of guy who does not get an offer on a drunk driving case. On one of his such cases, the client was clearly drunk, had in fact failed sobriety tests, and therefore was offered to plead straight up–which means no offer or "as charged." To John, this was an insult, and he got his client up in arms as a result. So, there they were, trying a case that no one had any business trying.

The morning of the trial, his client was offered an impaired driving. Under the facts of this dog case, this was a reduction in penalty and a was good offer. John took it to his client and got the thumbs down. Now, this is where John, and nearly all other lawyers, differ: John simply said to the prosecutor, "Let's let the jury decide." I would have broken my client's arms to take this deal. He was dead to rights and was on a motorcycle with a half a twelve pack strapped to the back of his seat. It was just within easy reaching distance. Are you kidding me?

"The state calls Officer Jason Matthews."

Officer Matthews then proceeded to explain in detail the perfect stop, presenting it with all the professionalism a seasoned trooper can muster. It was a compelling case and pointed, beyond a reasonable doubt, to drunk driving. It was simple. The motorcycle swerved. The motorcyclist smelled of intoxicating alcohol. His eyes were bloodshot, and he failed the preliminary breath test at the vehicle and the more sophisticated test at the station. It was an obvious open and shut case.

Not so fast.

John got up to bat and said, "Officer, I noticed that he had a 12 pack strapped to the back of his Harley Davidson Motorcycle. Is that correct?"

John loved those "Harley Davidson" type questions. He was a true wordsmith. Why use the word girlfriend when you could add some intrigue and call her a paramour? He was all about painting with his words to give the jury every visual possible.

Officer Matthews looked right at John and, without hesitation, said "that is correct, counsel."

A lot of cops hate lawyers, especially ones who do the following:

John asked, "Officer, how many beers were in the 12 pack?"

"Seven full beers were in there."

John wound up, pitched, and said, "What happened to the beer?"

Officer Matthews said, "I took it home."

The jury was out for 10 minutes, and the verdict was, not surprisingly, NOT GUILTY.

So odds are percentages also come with a grand caveat, the you-never-know caveat. We call this a revolving door jury. Usually that means revolving to kill our clients with a quick guilty. This, however, was a thing of beauty. It is called *jury nullification*. The jury did not care what the law was. They voted with their combined disgust for a police officer's taking the "evidence" home and drinking it. Well, John never asked if the officer had drank it. Hell no. This may have given him time to do an on-the-spot crafting of a savior story, like "I kept it there for overnight safe keeping." And since the prosecutor was new—cause that is what new prosecutors do to cut their teeth, try all sorts of driving-type cases—when asked if he had any follow up to John's cross-questioning, he said, probably thinking he did not want the officer to do more damage, "no further questions." Not asking any more questions is appropriate for a lawyer using new law school training. Law students are taught never to ask a question you do not know the answer to. Why? Simple. It keeps you from drowning in a witness going off on a tangent. Here, however, John got a plum. He was famous for always asking what he did not know the answer to. He could care less about the rulebook. He made up his own rules. The first rule in John's rulebook was "there ain't no rules." The sum total of everything he did was that, first and foremost, "the show must go on."

As an aside, if I were the prosecutor, I would have said something like this to the officer: "Officer you have been on the force for years, correct. You took the beer home, but you are not suggesting you tampered with evidence by drinking it?" This would have been a cue from the prosecutor to be careful with that take-it home answer. It would be an all or nothing approach. If the question had been asked and the officer had cleaned up the defense attorney's drubbing, the verdict would have been guilty. However, since the prosecutor already knew he had lost, might as well go for the gusto.

You can never know what will happen, and, sometimes, it is worth a shot to take a risk when you have nothing to lose. That is a cliché, having nothing to lose. These are the 'no offer' cases where you will get the same sentence no matter what. So, if you plead and are found guilty by a jury, it makes no difference. If, however, there is any benefit to pleading, by all means examine it closely. Your clients will never understand that they have a 90%+ chance of losing. Even with the worst case, your client will still sit in her cell with all the police reports and go line after line trying to piece together all the good stuff while ignoring all the bad. People can find 'the best case scenario' in the darkest places. Quite simply, it is more often than not, a fool's errand to try most cases.

Is there any really benefit to pleading straight up? Will the prosecutor agree on a sentencing cap? Will the court allow work release? These are tangible agreements and benefits that they most likely will not get after putting the whole system to work in a trial. Don't get me wrong; there are very real wins in the system, and they are most often found in settling the case on lesser charges. Mitigation is king in so much of the law when your client's liberty is in jeopardy. It is just that settling the case rather than going to trial is somehow unsatisfying for some client's because it seems to be the path of least resistance. Believe me, it is the path of greatest resolution for most cases.

Things like "you don't believe in me," and "you are working for the government," are the type of allegations that you live with and have to explain.

The grand point is that, sometimes, things happen at trial or in a motion or in any case, for that matter, that are completely unexpected.

You must keep your eye on the ball but your mind open. Take, for example, Rich, a friend of mine who is a career patrol police officer. Rich patrols the streets of a city large enough to have a president come to town. On one of the president's trips, Rich pulled president duty, which consisted of providing an armed presence downtown to aid the undercover secret service. The way the story goes, he was partnered with a secret service agent. They talked, of course, and he asked the agent how he liked his job. The agent replied that it was stressful, as his detail often had to leave home at a moment's notice, and that was hard for raising a family. Then he said,

"See those snipers on the roof of the taller buildings along the route the president's caravan will take?"

Rich responded, "I can't see all of them, but I assure you I know they are there."

The agent smirked a bit and said, "I don't want to alarm you, but one of them is assigned to point his high-powered rifle at you."

Rich gasped. "What in the hell? But I'm one of the good guys."

The agent said, "I'm sure you are most likely one of the good guys. The problem is that we do not know who might be carrying a gun—but we do know who *is* carrying a gun. So they are pointed at all the companion local uniformed and armed police for the president's protection."

Remember this point: You may be preparing for what you absolutely believe must be the route to success, But there are hundreds of routes, and many are as difficult to predict as this.

> It ain't what you don't know that gets you into trouble. It's what you know for sure that just ain't so.
>
> *Mark Twain*

Discussion Questions

1. Why does your client deserve your best guess, or odds of success?

2. How do you calculate odds? What components go into the equation?

3. When must you try a case?

4. Who should make the decision to go to trial: the lawyer, the client, or both?

5. Who makes the decision on whether to file motions and what motions to file?

PART III

Must Do!

CHAPTER 16

COUNT YOUR MONEY: A CAUTIONARY TALE

John had money everywhere. Once when I was trying a case with him, he found $1000 in his suit pocket. "Damn," he said, "I never wear this suit." As a starving young lawyer, I was envious. Not jealous, but new-lawyer-envious, the type of the envy that peers into the future and says, "That's me, alright, that's me!"

The only time I got unexpected money from the practice of law was when I was in church. Many years after working with John, I was attending a noon church ceremony at the local cathedral. Suddenly, the woman in front of me turns around at the end of mass, and I recognize her as the mother of a client from many years ago. She stood up to leave, but before she did, she shook my hand and said, "I owe this to you." In my hand was a piece of paper. In shock, I watched her walk away silently, and when I looked down at my hand, I saw that the piece of paper was in fact a check for $1000. I was dumbfounded. It must have been an outstanding bill she owed me. I chalked it up to the guilt she felt in court because I had forgotten all about it.

Whenever John called, it was always something good. He was over-run with cases and, as I said, he often shared them around.

"John would like to see you this afternoon," his super able assistant said.

Excitedly, I replied, "I'll be there!" And I was off in a flash.

John's office was grand. He was not the low-rent type of lawyer, although neither was he a silk stocking lawyer. He was his own man in his own firm.

He worked in one of those old-fashioned fire stations that had been transferred into a cool as hell law office. He had a huge stone fireplace and a mahogany desk the size of an ice skating rink. There was the crisp scent of leather throughout his office, and lawyer lamps were all over his conference room. His office looked like the library at the University of Michigan Law School or the courtyard at Northwestern. Yet he was no blue blood. John went to a law school just outside of Detroit, the Detroit College of Law, nicknamed DCL. It was a hard knocks law school that was liberal in its admissions policies. I never asked John how he did because after you pass the bar exam and get your law license, no one gives a shit how you did or where you went to law school. You are all in the same pool now. You're all lawyers with a license. And, as I have said before: "OK, GO!"

John was an 'OK-go,' type of guy. He had nothing to do with the established practice of law. He was a guy who knew he would excel because he had no fear. The prosecutor's great resources did not dissuade him. When he got a bad offer from the prosecutor, he would just say, "That's not gonna work." Plain and simple. The prosecutor knew what that meant: "See you at trial." John would say, "You may have the facts and the law, but I know jazz." And he did. No one could improvise like John, and when he would solo, it was a thing of beauty.

Let's go back to me. So I went in his office and found him staring at me over his desk. Then he said, "Got a couple of hours?" He paused and looked at an extern he was working with, paused again, and then said, half laughing, "a couple, profitable hours?"

"Sure," I responded, because if John said there was money, there was money. I had never been included in his inner sanctum of newer lawyers, but I had heard rumors that he could make you rich.

John stood up and said, "Come with me."

And with that, I found myself next in the passenger's seat of a top-of-the line Lexus. John changed cars like I changed underwear, and today, he had a Lexus. He never had it tricked out. He was 50 by the time I met him, and I was 35. He was all about business.

"Where are we going?"

"Benton Harbor, my man, Benton Harbor."

Then he explained that a family who wanted him to represent two cousins contacted him. I guess they were as close to identical twins as cousins could get. He called them "A-Z and I-Z, or, AZIZ." I guess to differentiate between them. I did not care about the story because he said it was an 'over 650 case' on both of them, and when I heard that, I stopped listening for a moment to count my money. 'Over 650,' at that time in Michigan, meant over 650 grams of cocaine. This was the magic number for police to permanently dispose of an individual because the penalty was life in prison without parole. This is called 'all day' in the criminal biz.

Needless to say, this was taken as seriously as a heart attack by the powers that be behind AZ and IZ, people who you didn't want to mess with. These were the type of people who would let 12-year-olds run crack rocks and mule the product all over the city. It really was a no-brainer, as the kids would be prosecuted as juveniles and would be allowed a number of arrests before they would do any time. But this was different—this was two young men in their late teens, and that was bad, real bad. The kind of bad that costs big money just to mitigate the damages. John was a ball-buster, and I was a mitigator, and there we were on our way for a meeting with Az and Iz and, of course, their 'people'.

We pulled up into the driveway of a two-story brown bungalow on one of the main streets of Benton Harbor. The house was in pretty good condition, but it was, as they say, on the bad side of town. There were couches on the porch and jars full of cigarette butts. It looked more like a flophouse or a fraternity than a cocaine dealership.

John said, "Follow my lead."

We walked up to the door, in suits, not sport coats but suits. Clients like their lawyers to wear suits especially when there is a lot of money involved. John told me on the way up that we were each getting

$20,000 at the meeting. I almost swallowed my tongue. "$20,000, " I said in a low breath, like you whisper holy shit! John looked back at me and said, "Welcome to the biggies."

With that, he knocked on the door. We walked into the living room, and instead of furniture, there was a big dining room table. No other furniture was in sight. The table was old, dented, and full of ashtrays. It was creepy.

An older African American man came into the room first and knuckled John's hand like he had done business with him before. And, indeed he had—the man was the father of one of the boys, IZ. He was no stranger to the law and had been to prison on numerous occasions. As prison by its own definition means anything over one year, he had been away a whole bunch.

So there I was, as white as a man in a KKK sheet, wondering how to shake hands coolly with a big African American drug dealer when I had no clue how to give the brother knuckle bump. I was just about to give it a Saturday Night Live white guy try when two more men came, so we all just sat down.

Champs was IZ's father. He had been a golden gloves champ in the Chicago projects where he grew up, Cabrini-Green, to be precise, a row of towering apartment complexes designed to house the un-houseable, those who had no money and no place to go. At its peak, it housed over 3,000 people, and it soon became a gang-infested cesspool. Champs was a success story from the Greens. He got into local YMCA-type fighting. He was gonna be somebody. He was a huge man and must have boxed heavyweight. He was as black as coal, and back then, which must be around 25 years ago, he was as muscular as you could be at 50.

"Let me tell you, Attorney Claussen (which was what African Americans tended to call lawyers), my boy and his cousin are in serious trouble, and they were set up."

Instead of responding, "How so?" John responded with a, "Firkin' cops! Jerk cops!" I wasn't a big fan but to not even hear the facts and already agree that it must have been a set up made me cringe. My whole world had been about dealing with and molding "client expectations."

If you tell them you are on-board from day one, where do you go from there?

Champs pulled out a sheet of paper and handed it to John. AZ had written it from his jail cell. You see, neither AZ or IZ could get bond. They were considered both a flight risk and a danger to the community, which are the standards used to evaluate bond, or the lack thereof. Sure, you *could* get a bond, but it was a weight on the pockets of the defendant bond. Here, each kid had a $500,000 cash bond. A cash bond means that you need to pay $500,000 in cash to get out and assure the court that you will make appearance or pay $50,000 to a bondsman—that you NEVER get back—and an additional amount of equity to cover the balance, which was not gonna happen for these two.

They almost got their boys out for the hundred that it would take, but they decided to spend more on lawyers and get them the best chance of winning because they had been, as Champs said, set up.

It should be obvious by now that when you hear the words "set up," the hairs on the back of your neck start to stand. It does that to a lawyer. It means we are paying a bunch of money, and we expect you to accept our legal conclusion as fact.

John looked at the note, and he put it between us so I could see it as well. It read:

Champs:

No powder, no money. Dudes gave a box of tide for a someday promise. No deal. No arrest.

AZ

John looked at me and asked, "Does that say what I think it says?"

Champs said, "Your mother F'en right it does. No product, no money, no case!"

"Wow," John said. "We have a war here. This is somma that old-fashioned cop bullshit."

I almost felt like the guys in the room were going to say "Amen, brother." But they didn't. They all just looked at me like they expected me to be the token white in a mostly-black county. They needed a serious-looking guy with glasses, a lily-white lawyer to say "bad boy" to the cops who hate blacks.

One of the guys in the other room walked in and said to me, "Lawyer, man, whatcha think? We winning this thing for our boys?"

"Holy shit," I thought. This is a bad place to be when you don't have the right answer. I mean how in the world could we promise a win? The defense wins a only small percentage of the time, and the day you believe your clients' relatives over a soon-to-be-seen-obviously-you're-guilty-as-hell police report is the day you do your work just to chase money and tempting a possible grievance from the State Bar of Michigan, or even worse, rough justice by an angry "family."

"Those cops will do anything to get your boys hung out to dry," John said, shaking his head in agreement with everything everyone said.

"Well, you got the secret weapons here, the cop's worst legal nightmare, out-a-town big timers!" I guess that meant us. Many clients in need of criminal defense lawyers believe that in-town attorneys are soft on the cops, as they have to work there day after day. Getting a lawyer from out of town, especially someone with a reputation, like John, was the ticket out of prison. At least I knew John would put up a hell of a fight. But win? Well, that is another question.

"So, tell us what the story is going to be." John asked, as if he wanted them to make something up. I remember sitting there for a moment feeling like I was going to be part or an illegal transaction. A criminal enterprise, like RICO, was unfolding. I could almost see the headlines:

EXTRA, EXTRA, READ ALL ABOUT IT:

LAWYERS INVOVED IN DRUG CONSPIRACY AND
CHARGED UNDER THE FEDERAL RACKETEERING STATUTE

Almost instantly, as if he had read my mind, John clarified his sentence and said: "Make sure it is the 100% truth. We can't work with made up lies."

The problem with clients' stories is that you quickly find out that there are three sides to a story: yours, mine, and the one that really happened. Let's face it: have five people write down about the same situation, and you will get five different versions of the same thing, not five of the same story. Plus, the longer you lawyer, the easier it is to tell a bullshit story. But, as the old saying goes, "Your eyes may sparkle and your teeth may glitter, but don't bullshit the ole bullshitter."

Champs continues, "It's the gods-honest truth that the boys were tryin' to scam the Feds. They had a line that the Feds were taking down Benton Harbor boys in Detroit by tricking them into bringing just enough white to get the boys an all-day trip, ya dig?" He paused and looked for approval from his compatriots. "They were just hookin' in by playing the game. They filled up a box of Tide with a false bottom and filled the bottom with a mix of baking soda and any white stuff they could muster. THEY COULD HAVE MADE A CAKE WITH THE STUFF THEY BOUGHT." Everybody in the room laughed with approval.

It turns out the plan was to arrange the delivery of the cake mixture to undercover vice agents at a McDonald's in Detroit near the Renaissance Center. They met the undercover in Benton Harbor, where they did sell a real batch of sample cocaine for a few hundred dollars with a promise to bring nearly 1,000 grams to Detroit. To put this into perspective. A 100 grams is a kilo of cocaine, or 2.2 pounds. The "lifer" law in Michigan was over 650 grams of product. It was intended to get the biggest of the big but it really was a small quantity for this incredibly disproportionate penalty. AZ and IZ were, by no stretch of the imagination, "kingpins." The boys went to great length to make the transaction look real. (The undercover, by the way, had been introduced to them by a customer who had recently been busted and was trying to buy his time down snitching on a couple of sellers he called the "biggies" to impress the cops.) The transaction occurred in Sturgis Michigan, so they were completely unknown to the buyer. The snitch was not even there. He just arranged things so it would look like he had introduced them. Things like three lights from the Walgreens on Matt St. Everyone did a pretty good job of unanimity, even in the nickel and dime world of drugs.

AZ and IZ went to Detroit in two separate cars. One was going to be a lookout set up across the street, and the other was going to just lay low. IZ did have a gun, but he was not going to use it under most circumstances. The undercover buyer was to have a Detroit Tigers bobble-head in his back window on the driver's side. The plan was that one of them would go up to the car, which should be empty, place the package in the backseat, and pick up the $10,000 down payment on a $15,000 deal. They were fronting the rest, which, of course is a no-win proposition. However, if you are basically stealing the 10k, who cares?

AZ parked his car in the lot after seeing a white Chevy Impala with tints sitting a few cars away from him. He wanted to be as close as possible and to scope things out before he dropped the Tide. As was later seen on video in court, he got out of his car, without bringing the Tide, walked over to the Chevy, checked to see that the money was in the back seat, and then walked very briskly back to his car to get the box. As had been pre-arranged, he flashed his brights, and IZ flashed back. Then he walked back toward the Chevy. The moment he opened the door, the video was triggered in the car, and as he set the box down on the backseat and grabbed the money bag, he immediately found himself surrounded by 10 vice cops screaming:

"Hands on your head! Hands on your head!"

At the same moment, there were another half dozen vice cops yelling the very same thing at IZ across the street. The night was full of panic and pandemonium, and it was pitch black, except for the glow of the golden arches. There were cops running everywhere, taking IZ's gun, and screaming, "Take the coke, grab the monopoly money, get his gun." The exchange hadn't even taken a few minutes, but in an instant, it was over. Busted.

In the criminal business, everyone is lying. AZ and IZ were not biggies. They were not kingpins. They were rock sellers, nickel and dimmers. But there they were in lock-up with a million in total bond and a snitch who had probably bought off his case because of the set-up. Now, after hearing the story, we knew why they had been charged with Conspiracy to Distribute Cocaine over 650 grams. What they did, in essence, was just that. Did it matter that they did not have any cocaine at all? Probably not. Was the intent to sell imaginary cocaine enough to charge? Did the cop know it was imaginary? Was the fact that the money was not real relevant? So, was this a case of a couple of hoods selling baking soda for monopoly money? Should they be in jail forever?

"Twenty thousand dollars each, as we discussed," John boomed. It was as though he was saying, "Let us be the lawyers. We have business to attend to, and that is saving your boys' lives."

With that, another even scarier black dude, came out of some room that I had thought was a bedroom or a vault. He plopped right in front of us a stack of 100s, one in front of John and one in front of me. "Holy shit," I was thinking. "This is more cash than I have ever seen in my life."

They looked over at me with a combined, "Who the hell is this guy?" look. "Gonna count it?" Champs asks. "Naw," I said as though this made me one of the guys. You know, the trusting one who would never be deceived by a bunch of cocaine dealers with $40,000 in cash.

I looked over at John and saw him counting using his lips. He touched every hundred. "$4,800, $19,400, $20,000. All here."

John then took the two stacks and put them in back in the bags, and we each put one in our briefcases.

As we got into John's car, I was, frankly, petrified. I mean, $20,000 is great but was someone going to follow us now? Was the house staked out? Were there wires being worn? But, who cares about wires? We were just listening to a story. We were only there an hour, and in that hour, we walked away with a lot of money and a veiled promise to solve their problems. AZ and IZ were in good hands, but how much good could we do with the entire police force from several communities involved in testifying to the Drug Conspiracy. I thought, "Come on. No drugs, no money, no case, right?"

John opened the glove compartment and said, "Put the money in here. But before you do, count your money."

I asked, "Why?"

John pulled away and said, "Count."

Five minutes later, John said, "So, whatcha got?" I remember feeling like an idiot when I said "$19,100." John smiled and said. "Now, how ya gonna get your money?"

Lesson learned.

DISCUSSION QUESTIONS

1. Why was not counting the money ill-advised? How were you going to get it at a later date?

2. What does this chapter tell you or warn you about expectations?

3. Discuss why you can have problems with more than just your client if you do not manage everyone's expectations.

4. Can you fee share with a lawyer in a criminal matter for recommending you to a client who retains you? What are the ethical ramifications of this?

5. What do you do if you lose and the family asks for their money back?

CHAPTER 17

THE DREADED GRIEVANCE

A grievance is a complaint to the state bar about something you did as an attorney or something you failed to do. Face it, not everybody is going to be happy with you all the time, but some can be militant about it. Many lawyers think getting a grievance is the end of the world. It is not. It is only the end of the world, legally speaking, if you ostrich it. This is not time to put your head in the sand. You must answer the allegations and on time. Period. It is the star chamber of the profession, and the people there play for keeps. Certain grievances are no-brainers, using a client's money (proceeds from a case), coming to work in court drunk, or calling the opposing party's client a bitch to her face. You almost deserve what you get when you behave this way.

I was on the Standing Committee for Attorney Grievances in the State of Michigan. In my time there, I learned something very valuable: The vast majority of grievances are for divorce lawyers and criminal defense lawyers; this dwarfs all others. Thus, if you become a street lawyer, you have to expect this to happen at some point. In the federal system, there is a statute that is commonly called 2255. This is the federal form of grievance.

I once was grieved because I did not finish a divorce in six months. Now, the full story was that I told a client that the divorce required a six-month waiting period to complete. In Michigan, if you have children, you must wait six months from filing the divorce before you end it. It took seven, although it usually takes far longer. My client filed a grievance on a divorce I did lickety-split. She must have thought it had to be done by month six, and she never mentioned it to me. I have worked on divorces that lasted two years, so seven months is fast. When the letter came, it looked like a certified letter from the IRS. I couldn't imagine it to be anything pleasant. In fact, the envelope was marked Attorney Grievance Commission. "Damn," you will say out loud when you see it. Inside, you will see that someone has filed a grievance against you as follows: They will usually attach the form they had to fill out and ask you for a response. Many times, it will say no response required. Then it is a letter addressed to the complaining party saying they will not pursue it. Like the time a federal prisoner who received 30 years in prison grieved me for not "pursuing his divine rights under the constitution for cruel and unusual punishment."

But this is all part of the life of a lawyer. Not everyone is going to like you or your work. It is inevitable, and do not let it throw you. If you looked in your state's bar journal, you will see that most of them are resolved short of license suspension, which is life-changing. The most common mistake in handling these is NOT answering their inquiry. It is a must-do.

I represented a lawyer who received a grievance after being convicted of a crime. He was a well-known lawyer in his county and was a bomb-thrower in the court system. The prosecutors hated him and rejoiced when he was arrested for drinking too much and pushing his wife of 40 years. It was a bad idea. Not only did the county prosecutor want the death penalty, he would not negotiate the spouse abuse—every doing gets one bite exception to the crime. It meant that if my client did a small probation and some counseling, which he needed, he would be able to have a clean record. To avoid the public embarrassment of a trial, he plead without much of a deal, except no jail. He would tell you today, "I did it, and you pay for your choices." (Perfect thing to say in court, by the way).

This is a part of practice that is inevitable, like paying malpractice insurance every year. Malpractice and grievances are quite different. A grievance is made to the State Bar Association complaining about something the client believed was a miss, like stealing their money. Truth be told though, most grievances are more about clients who do not like losing and need to blame someone. Malpractice is an actual lawsuit where you are sued for harming a client. These are common, and there are lawyers who specialize in handling them. They are good at tripping lawyers, and a completely different animal than a grievance.

The first thing you do, even if there is a threat of a lawsuit—let's say, for example, you blew a statute of limitations. It happens—is that you call the insurance carrier. Remember, they are experts at not paying claims. The phrase is "putting them on notice." These are magic words, and doing it is required, but many lawyers do not "tell them" until it is too late because they do not want a black mark on their record. The fear is that "What if a lawsuit does not unfold, now the insurance carrier has a note in the file that I have been threatened?" Big deal.

I was the managing partner in a ten-lawyer law firm. We had about 25 employees, with lawyers, and we thought we were the shit. We were a very good firm and represented some big clients with big cases. In one such case, we were contacted by a nurse who believed she was involved in a breach of contract with a major hospital that kept changing the terms of her contract. This eventually led to a lawsuit against the hospital, where we represented 52 nurses who were similarly situated.

We battled the hospital for five years, and the matter went to the court of appeals twice and the state supreme court once during the case. It was all-out war. We learned a lot about managing expectations with 52 people with 52 different claims. It was a management extravaganza. We tried the case and won the issue of liability. All that was left were damages. We presented detailed spreadsheets on the losses of each and every nurse. The hospital baulked. They did this partially because the supreme court in our state was very friendly to businesses, especially big businesses.

Finally, the hospital made us an offer to settle. It was a decent offer, and we were glad to accept it because we were all war-weary. The judge called all 52 nurses into court and told them, "You better take this; you could lose it all on appeal." Everyone agreed except two. The peer pressure was absolutely staggering. The two were pillared, and they ultimately signed the settlement agreement saying "We understand and agree to this settlement and this matter is resolved at this time." Amen.

Not so fast. A little less than two years later, they sued the firm for malpractice. "Huh?" We had won the trial, and they had agreed to the settlement. The suit was dismissed fairly quickly, but it goes to show that you need malpractice insurance. Again, this is a must. Had we not had it, geeze. I used to teach students, "Anyone can sue anytime for anything." It does not matter whether the accusation is valid or not, that's just a fact.

We got cards and letters and phone calls from the happy nurses. The two who sued us probably wanted never to work another day in their life because they had been wronged. This is not how lawsuits work, and I guess we were unsuccessful at explaining that. It is interesting to note that I saw one of the two who sued us years later at an Apple store. I was with my youngest son, and she walked up to me and said, "I forgive you." Since I am pretty quick-witted and this was just ridiculous, I said, "For what, winning?"

Then there is the "There but for the grace of God," section of your state's bar magazine. It is a list of all state actions regarding attorneys who have come to court drunk or have failed to return due money to a client—or even worse, because it is so dumb, failed to answer a grievance. Since most of the grievances filed with the state grievance commission are dismissed offhand, they are only a real problem if you are a criminal, not diligent in your reply, or are in denial. The ostrich approach will not work in this business. It's like putting off a root canal. Guess what happens in both scenarios?

28 USC § 2255 of the federal system seems like it would be an automatic. It curtails a lot of things the Defendant is complaining about, but one of them is ineffective assistance of counsel. I don't want to go all legal on you, but let me explain the 2255.

The long form of the title of the motion is, "Motion under 28 U.S.C. § 2255 to Vacate, Set Aside, or Correct Sentence by a Person in Federal

Custody." It is commonly referred to as a "collateral attack on the judgment," as opposed to a direct appeal, which is a "direct attack on the judgment." It is a type of post-conviction motion. 28 U.S.C. § 2255 and § 2241 make up the old *habeas corpus* law.

It is commonly used for more than ineffective assistance of counsel; it is also used for prosecutorial misconduct, newly-discovered evidence, or a substantive change in the law. As an attorney, when you hear 2255, you don't really have to worry. Frankly, it is not as serious as a state grievance because of a few very interesting things. First, 2255s are very common cut and paste motions. Prisoners in the federal system, on average, get five plus years. Do you think they are happy to be there? Do you think they are going to blame their incarceration on themselves? Please. It will be your fault or the prosecutor's fault. As a result, they will borrow the motion filed by the guy in the cell next to him, find a way to cut and paste, and voila! You have a brand new-looking motion that says the same thing the courts summarily reject. Just because it looks like a motion does not mean it is. Prisoners, by and large, do not know how to do these whatsoever. Second, and most curious, if the 2255 is about ineffective assistance of counsel, guess who represents you? The United States Attorney's Office. That's right. The same attorney who prosecuted your client now pounds his chest, saying what an effective job you did. It is just delicious when you think about it.

The bottom line is that even if the prisoner wins the 2255, the remedy is not that he or she can go home. It can be a new trial or a new sentence, but they are rare and usually not fruitful for the defendant. Defendants do, however, get a lot of mail from the court marked REJECTED. Because, after all, even though they are not lawyers, the court still holds to the same rules that lawyers use and if you violate them, too bad.

Discussion Questions

1. Why is the head in the sand approach to an attorney grievance the worst possible thing to do?

2. Are the words "you agree not to grieve me" in a fee agreement effective?

3. Why should you not panic when you receive a grievance?

4. What practice areas get the most grievances? Why?

5. What is the difference between a malpractice suit and a grievance?

CHAPTER 18

BREAKDOWN OF THE ATTORNEY CLIENT RELATIONSHIP

If the previous chapter did not give you a perfect example of a breakdown in the attorney client relationship when you have 52 client's with similar grievances but different objectives, I do not know what will. It had all the elements of one, but the breakdown didn't happen because clients like winning trials. They just think that they should win the lotto as well. If you want to see what this feels, like watch the movie *Civil Action* with John Travolta. We nearly bankrupted ourselves in the 52 nurse case. You cannot say, "We're out of money. We need to stop now." You need to slog on, and if you have a client who his not onboard, you need to make changes.

There was an attorney who had a particularly difficult criminal client who was looking at some serious time. (I define serious time as anything over ten years in prison.) He had a tumultuous relationship with his client, and it was obvious during the trial that his lawyer held contempt for him. Their relationship became so bad that every day before the trial began, right before the jury was called in, the defendant, who is allowed to be un-handcuffed in front of the jury, would stand up right as the officer would undo his handcuffs and say, "I don't want this shit lawyer anymore." The judge, who was not one for nonsense in his courtroom, was patient, and he would just tell him that if had any more outbursts like than in front of the jury, he would be placed in lock up and could just watch his trial by video. Then he would add, "Motion for a new attorney, denied. Bailiff, bring in the jury."

At about day four of the trial, it was obvious the defendant had enough. He was sitting there trying to look disruptive, but this was more act than actual. You're allowed to wear street clothes if you are a Defendant so you do not look so guilty—nothing makes you look guiltier than being in jail orange and sitting next to a defense attorney. All of a sudden, out of nowhere, the defendant stood up and hit his defense lawyer square in the face, breaking two teeth and his jaw. Immediately, the courtroom was in bedlam, and the jury was ushered out briskly on an emergency basis.

Two days later, the defense attorney, all bandaged up, returned. He quickly made a motion for a mistrial, and the prosecution objected, saying, "We cannot let an unruly defendant control this court's docket."

Then the defense attorney said, "It goes without saying, your honor, that I want an order allowing me to withdraw as counsel of record. There has certainly been a breakdown of the attorney-client relationship."

To this, the judge, a well-respected member of the bench, leaned back in his chair comfortably and said, "Motion denied to both motions. We will proceed as if nothing happened."

The defense attorney blasted back, "I just spent two days in the hospital because of this nut, and you want me to continue?"

The judge said, "Counsel, we will protect you at all costs. Can you imagine what would happen if I allowed all these shenanigans at this point? Every single defendant awaiting trial would know how to get a new lawyer or a mistrial."

The lesson here is powerful. Judges do not like to change horses. I have been in courtrooms when a lawyer has to come in hat in hand and say, "My client has stopped communicating with me, and I need an adjournment on Monday's trial."

The judge would say, "With all due respect, counsel, I cannot let your client's failure to live up to his responsibilities grind the wheels of justice to a halt."

There are many ways to get off of a case, and they are mostly to do with timely filing and appropriate reasons. The judge will be far more amenable if it is done three months before the trial, as opposed to three days. It is critical to remember that the court runs on a very tight schedule. This schedule is so tight that getting a new lawyer many times requires an adjournment of some sort, and maybe even a new scheduling order. It is a lot of running around, and the court does not like wasting time.

Probably the worst excuse for getting off of a case, which is called a Motion to Withdraw Appearance, is because you are not getting paid. This is your problem, not the courts', and if you are not good enough at making business arrangements, that's too bad. This is true even if you have a fee agreement that allows you to withdraw. Remember, the court is not subject to the terms of that agreement.

Discussion Questions

1. Why does it matter to the court whether you, not another lawyer, tries the case?

2. Shouldn't the case where the lawyer was injured automatically have been a mistrial? Wouldn't it be reversed on appeal? Why didn't the judge care?

3. Is there a way to write a fee agreement that would allow you to withdraw if you do not receive payment?

4. How do you handle a trial wherein your client just does not show up? Some clients believe that if they do not show up, it will be cancelled.

5. Why is it important to be careful what you write in your Motion to Withdraw? Think about the ethical considerations.

CHAPTER 19

You're Not in the Circus,
But You'll Sure Learn to Juggle

On Lincoln: *First, he developed and learned the need for unending energy especially when considering that Lincoln expended equal, concurrent energy in politics. Second, his legal-political career demonstrated that Lincoln had the ability to juggle effectively more than one job at the same time. Third, the study of law and his work in the legislature allowed him to develop and hone his political skills. Fourth, the law allowed him to develop his ability as a public speaker and writer. Fifth, the law also gave him time to reflect on human nature and the broader purpose of democratic life. Ultimately, Lincoln's dual careers provided him the kind of broad background that assured him the potential for growth as a politician, which was always his ultimate goal. It would ensure that not only would he be a commander in chief or an attorney in chief but also he would evolve as America's finest political leader. Sixth, his legal casework taught him a great sense of timing, knowing when to undertake an issue directly and when to be Machiavellian."*

Frank J. Williams, Judging Lincoln, p. 37.

Most lawyers I know are not purists. Even if they specialize in one field of law, they still tend to dabble in other things like teaching, public speaking, boards of directors, township appointments and the like. Add to this possibly raising children, and God forbid, having a life, and you have a full-time professional at several things all at the same time and on several levels.

It is a circus, but you need to control by putting a tent around it. Early on, I told you about the mega firm lawyer who got burnt out to the point of a death at 52. When researching this book, I could not even find an obituary for him. His grand accomplishments in the law ultimately amounted to saving a few big corporations some money. He did not cure the common cold or help the local food pantry to thrive. He just did lots and lots of paperwork and died. Pretty much the end.

What he did for a living was being a litigator. Litigators are often confused with trial lawyers. Nothing could be further from the truth. A trial lawyer is a lawyer who does trials. Prosecutors and public defenders are trial lawyers. It is a rare lawyer in the so-called big firms who is a true trial lawyer. This is not to belittle the role of the litigator in the litigation process. They are fine lawyers who solve cases through a series of legal maneuvering or alternate dispute resolution (ADR)— meaning, not trial. They are, by and large, paper lawyers who try cases through the mail. So, as it goes in the trial business, he was the lesser of two evils.

One of the other partners in the big firm used to say all the time, "I have a lot of work to do before my heart attack." Now, imagine that statement coming out of your mouth. Imagine the idea that life has become that sarcastically desperate. I have watched lawyers run and run to the point of oblivion because, if the truth be told, law firms will let you work yourself to death if you want. Heck, there is always another lawyer.

It all comes down to priorities. Yet, in the end, everything does. This is especially true in those all-consuming careers. One of the best lawyers I knew by way of priorities was Charlie D. Charlie was an environmental attorney who graduated from a top school. As a close friend of my father, who was a federal judge, he once told me, "Your degree gets you your first job. All else, you must prove yourself." Charlie was the kind of guy who never had to worry about having to get that second job. In a career that is many times transitory, staying for more than five years could entitle you to a gold watch.

His work ethic was unsurpassed. He would get in everyday at 7:00 a.m. By the time I swaggered in at 8:30, it almost seemed that Charlie was ready for lunch. He then ate at his desk at 11:00. By 3:00, he was turning off his light, closing his door, and calling it a day. No one batted an eye because Charlie billed his eight, and it was top quality work. Charlie did not socialize, but he never turned down any request to answer a question. He was one of those guys who would stop everything, look you straight in the eye, and wait until you completed your question. He was a true gentleman, and everyone admired him. He would regularly bill a true 1800 hours a year, and that was about 3x his salary. This was a profit source, and they knew it. The rest of us played games like leaving lights on and coming every Saturday, staying just long enough to be seen and we were out of there. Not Charlie. He was the real deal. People can tell whether you are a climber, a game player, or a Charlie. It is just obvious, and even though they may not say anything to your face, they know what you are.

Now let's take a look at another type of lawyer I'll call Steve:

At the big firm, in the office next to mine was a young Hispanic woman named Terese. Terese was a brilliant law student and sure to be a brilliant lawyer. She was assigned a mentor named Steve. Steve was a Yale grad, and he would tell you that halfway through his morning donut. Every day. He was a social climber, and worst of all, he was a vicious climber at the firm. Climbing at a law firm of any size is a career in itself. It takes cunning, skill, a pedigree, and the lack of a conscience. It is pretty easy to take the wrong step, and the only thing easier is to burn out. Associates put in thousands of hours before they are even recognized as valuable. And a great deals of those hours are just tossed aside by the partner who assigned the hours.

Now Terese was fragile. She was a hard worker and loved the work, but she was a a mom first and then a lawyer. This was back when being a lawyer needed to be your #1, and then you would squeeze your family in whatever space was left. Hopefully, you had an understanding spouse because lawyers were not on track to have a normal life for at least 10 years. Terese was not completely into this program, and she sensed that her associate mentor did not smell blood like a good litigator must. Terese also had a partner mentor who was the opposite of her tyrannical associate mentor. Isn't that always the way? The ones at the top so often send the elevator down when they get there for others to rise. But this partner had no clue that Terese was being bullied.

It was 5:45, and most of the partners were leaving. But it was a Thursday night, and so all of the associates were staying. The usual call-it-quits time was 7:00, and then home. Terese usually left at 6. But today was different; Steve had to go out of town on a bigshot case. Like the sadistic bastard that he was, he decided to set her up in front of a slow-moving freight train. He gave her an assignment that had to be filed by noon the next day so it could be heard the next week. That is legal jargon for filing a motion and letting the other side know in enough time to respond and show up. From what I saw, she must have worked all night on the motion. She got it filed by noon and then went home to sleep.

That Monday morning, I got to the office at 7:00. Terese's door was closed, and I could hear talking and pleading. After a few minutes, Steve left the room. I walked past her office several times, and I did not get a rise from her, but I could see through her window that she was sobbing. I was furious. I thought to let her alone, but instead of busting in, I finally decided to just knock. It turns out that Steve had come in over the weekend, found the motion, and taken the time to slice it apart. He had made so many changes to it it it looked like someone had spilled red paint all over it. And these were all just style changes, not legal changes or typos. I mean, come on! It devastated her. And the worst of it was that this idiot made her incorporate all of the changes, make an appointment with the judge, withdraw and reschedule the motion, and show the judge the bad copy and the new improved asshole copy.

I happened to be far older than most of the associates, so I confronted him. I told him to leave her alone. I told him to pick on someone his own size. I told him he was a bully. I am sure it led to my inevitable demise at the firm a few years later. But I will never forget the lesson I learned after that: Law is a blood sport. I received a call about a week later from a voice I did not recognize. The caller said, "Lock your files." Lock your files meant someone was going to tamper with them, like lose the pleadings or destroy evidence. It meant someone was out to get me. I wonder who?

Do you think everyone knew about what Steve did? Sure they did. When Terese was summoned to the partner's office after Steve turned her in and tried to look better to the world by making her look worse, what do you think her partner-mentor thought? You got it, he was thinking that Steve was an jerk, not that Terese was a bad lawyer. She was brand-new, for the love of God, and Steve should have known better than to dump a big project on her at the last minute with no real guidance or supervision.

The associates hated him. He thought he was all that and a bag of chips because his degree was from Harvard. The reason I mention his degree again is because he really went to Wayne State and just transferred to Harvard. We use to call him a Wayne State dropout.

Your lot in life will be about balancing all of the various matters of politics. It is a "who you go to lunch with" world. My wife and I were once invited to a summer cookout by one of the partners at the big firm. This partner was someone I really did not know, and I was pleased to be included in a very small list. I got to the party and found out that she had chosen me out of a hat. The partners had all been required to invite a newbie, and guess who the lucky guy was? At some level, it was still a fun party, but at another, forced friendship or socialization? Come on.

The juggling does not stop at work/family. It happens daily and every decision you make. For example, let's say you have two hearings on Friday. Both are in the same courthouse, and one is at 10 while the other is at 11. You have an empty calendar after. So, the whole day, you are free. But these two hearings could cause a years' worth of stress. First, the 10 o'clock one does not start till 10:20, and then you need to leave at 10:50 to get to the other on time. At about 10:00, you ask the clerk to alert the 11 o'clock courtroom that you are running late. Then when it hits 11:10, you know you have a whole courtroom just sitting and waiting and they do not know (or care) that this courtroom was running late due to NO fault of your own. Geeze.

DISCUSSION QUESTIONS

1. The lawyer's disease is overwork. Discuss balance and what you plan to do to balance your career and life.

2. How do you attend a child's ballgame and a trial scheduled at the same time?

3. Some people choose partnership over family early on in their career. Is this a good choice when you are in the early stages of your career?

4. Why is it good to set boundaries and expectations with yourself or your employer?

5. Why do you think many lawyers call the circuit court the circus court?

CHAPTER 20

Reputation: It's up to You

Lincoln: There is a vague popular belief that lawyers are necessarily dishonest. I say vague because when we consider to what extent confidence and honors are reposed in and conferred upon lawyers by the people, it appears improbable that their impression of dishonesty is very distinct and vivid. Yet the impression is common, almost universal. Let no young person choosing the law for a calling for a moment yield to the popular belief---resolve to be honest at all events; and if in your own judgment you cannot be an honest lawyer, resolve to be honest without being a lawyer.

Mr. Lincoln's caseload ranged from the criminal to the corporate, from the petty to the principled. Historian Cullom Davis wrote: "Lincoln had a much larger and more widely diversified general practice than generally recognized. Lincoln was an aggressive and tenacious litigator whose mastery of civil and criminal procedure surfaced frequently. Popular notions about his carelessness and homespun demeanor tend to obscure a tough streak in his pre-trial and courtroom tactics. Neither flowery nor bombastic, he nevertheless frequently sought continuances, changes of venue, and dismissals on technical grounds when it was to his client's advantage. He could, as historian Robert Bruce aptly put it, 'split hairs as well as rails.'" 32 Cullom Davis, Abraham Lincoln and the Gold Age of American Law, p. 9, 12.

This goes hand in hand with the "there are too many lawyers" rap. They are both false. I am by no means the gold standard in understanding lawyer behavior, but I can tell you that of the few hundred I know, they are, by and large, some of the most hardworking and honest people I know. The idea that lawyers are dishonest must come from the idea that every single case has a winner and a loser, and that equation alone tells you that there are people angry at some lawyer in every case. People hate to lose, and when they do, it certainly can't be their fault. It must be the lawyer's fault. I mean, who else's?

This image, however, must be cultivated lawyer by lawyer. Your reputation should be crafted using the finest of values. These include honesty, punctuality, cleanliness, respect, competency, hard work ethic, temperament, and honor. These are cultivated throughout your life, and you should probably have a good grasp on them by the time you hit law school. Just the idea of trudging your way through a bachelor's degree with all the testing required and all the scheduling and public speaking and more testing and honor codes than you've seen in your life and you have a stand-up life being organized all around you.

There are lawyers who will lie to your face and lie in court. It is then when your reputation is on full display. The judge takes the sum total of everything he or she knows about you in each and every one of your appearances. If you are known to be loose with the truth, it will surely be reflected in how the court reacts and treats you.

One of my best examples deals with a very seasoned attorney from the prosecutor's office. I had a client in his late 20s, let's call him Robert, who was arrested and charged with Criminal Sexual Conduct against his two-year-old daughter. A horrifying charge, but that's just the beginning of the story. Robert was a well-paid employee of a major office furniture manufacturer. He had been married to his wife, Alice, for nearly 10 years, and they had two children, a six-year old son and a two-year-old daughter. Both parties wanted full custody of the children, and, as customary, the court referred the case for a custody evaluation. The custody evaluation came down on the side of the father, and out of the blue, Alice called the custody evaluator and told him that she had failed to mention that Robert had sexually molested his daughter.

When words like "sexually molested" come to the attention of people in the legal or medical business, they are required under law to report it to the authorities and make no independent evaluation of whether the facts seem valid. The idea is that even though they may be a pediatrician, or something like that, they are not in a position to judge the truth or falsity of an allegation. There are pros for that.

Quick, stop the presses! The quickest way to destroy a relationship with a child is to bring in sexual allegations. That call by Alice started a multi-year litigation matter in criminal court, as well as neglect court. At every turn, the authorities believed the child, and there are no doubts that the father is guilty. The little girl said to a forensic investigator only one sentence, "Daddy put a cigarette in my butt." That is all she said. No more and no less. But it was enough to get the father charged with first-degree sexual abuse. At this time in the 1990s, it did not matter whether the father smoked and may have dropped an ash on her while changing a diaper, because, after all, folks, men do change little girl's diapers. They are dads, for the love of God. It does not matter that Alice had just lost a custody evaluation. All these seemed superfluous. Yet, to a lawyer, they were critical aspects of a case that had all the smacking's of being contrived to tip the scales of custody into mom's favor.

At the first hearing, the prosecutor listened to my spin and tended to agree with me. Since the accused (not the victim, for those adult victim cases) has the right to a non-admissible polygraph, we agreed that my client would take a poly. I asked him if he would dismiss the case he passed, and he said, and I quote verbatim, "If he passes, we aren't going anywhere with it."

It is true that polygraphs are not admissible, BUT they are a good tool for prosecutors to use against their own client: the victim. Really, their client is the state, but in effect, they are dealing with just one person, or one family. The reason the law allows defendant's to take a poly when they are not admissible is because sex crimes are usually "he said, she said" crimes. These are hard to decipher with adults who may both have believable stories. If the defendant passes, the prosecutor can then say to the victim, "he passed, and this makes it hard to prosecute." But what he or she is really saying is that you're probably the liar.

Even though this was suppose to be about the custody and safety of a little girl, her mother made it all about winning custody and getting her soon-to-be, ex-husband prosecuted for molesting their daughter. And what better way to win custody forever and always than to put him in prison? Just another parting gift to celebrate the end of their tumultuous marriage and divorce. She did not care about child support because she was a major executive at the same company he worked at, and guess what? He got fired because of this.

[Lawyer tip: Have your client take a private polygraph with a very experienced polygraph operator. You will have no trouble finding the go-to guy who recently retired from the state police and is at the top of the pyramid in lie detector examination. It is worth the money. But before you go pounding on your chest that your client takes one, make sure he will pass. This is an excellent insurance policy. If he passes, demand that he takes a state-administered poly. If he flunks, be righteously indignant about the audacity of the state to even offer it. Then if he flunks the state's poly and you already have results that he passed with an even more experienced polygraph operator, you, at least, have zeroed out the result. If it is a clear fail and you have no ammunition, then you're screwed. The prosecutor will now be sure you're guilty, and your bargaining power will go even further down.]

He passed the polygraph. It was a clear pass. So, I went about the business of contacting the prosecutor.

"Is Steve B. in?"

"I'll take a message."

Over a span of three weeks, I made call after call, but Steve B. was never in. And he never called back. It was like the old lawyer joke about an insurance adjustor's failure to return his calls, "If the phone doesn't ring, I'll know it's you."

I finally passed him on the street, and he said "I'm sorry I didn't call you back. Stacy (the head of the sex crimes department) took over the case." Stacy was a good lawyer. She was a hard charger from the prosecutor's office, but she was known for bending the truth on occasion.

I said, "What the hell does that mean?"

It meant, he said, "She won't let me dismiss the case."

I thanked him, and we gave each other that certain lawyer look, like there is far more to the story but "I ain't tellin'," and walked on.

I immediately called Stacy, who told me I must have misunderstood the former prosecutor on the case. To this, I filed a Motion to Enforce Prosecutor's Agreement. Look it up, there is such a thing. It it was beautiful, and it worked.

On the day of the hearing, Steve B. was called to the stand:

"You were the original prosecutor on this case."

"Yes."

"Isn't it true that you told defense counsel that if his client passed the polygraph that you, and I quote, 'would not be going anywhere with this case?'"

"Yes."

"Defense counsel believed that meant that you would dismiss the case. What did it mean to you?"

"The same"

"That you dismiss?"

"Yes."

"But you did not, correct?"

"Correct."

"Why not?"

"I was told not to by my superiors."

"No more questions, your honor."

The court dismissed the case with an admonition to the prosecutor's office.

Discussion Questions

1. If you plan to move around, why does reputation matter? Let's face it, if you practice in one county or state, how would your reputation follow you anyway?

2. What did the senior prosecutor do wrong in this case?

3. What did the junior prosecutor do right when he took the stand?

4. Should lawyers be sanctioned for bad behavior? Unethical behavior?

5. Discuss how you could have resolved this matter.

CHAPTER 21

50 Tips for Practicing Law

This advice may not be from a sage or a wise man, but I've collected these tips over the years, has and they have suited many students well. Going through this is a quick reminder of how many things to consider when practicing law.

TIP 1: LEARN HOW TO READ THE JURY.
I regularly sit silently when the jury rings the buzzer to tell the court that they have reached a verdict. The door from the jury room opens into the courtroom, and when they begin the slow procession to take their places, I always look at their eyes. If they will not look at the Defendant, it is bad news.

TIP 2: NEVER HAVE WHAT THE JURY DOES NOT.
This mostly relates to coffee (which most courts do not allow) or especially water. Imagine being in the jury and watching as the cool attorney across from you sips cool water while you are sweating from the stress. Nice, huh?

TIP 3: MINIMIZE DISTRACTIONS.
It goes without saying but never chew gum or anything in court. Are you kidding me? That's disrespectful. It's like wearing a hat in court—you will be pillared. Your phone better be on full silent as well. It you

accidently hit some app and a bell goes off, you're toast. The judge will tell you, "Either you or your phone will be in jail for the weekend."

TIP 4: DON'T DRESS LIKE A SLOB.

Dress like someone is paying you a lot of money because most of the time, they are. Ladies, dress like a business professional. This topic is hard for an older man to talk about, but let me just say that court is not about looking good or getting favors because of what you are wearing. That's lawyer speak for please cover up. Both men and women should blend in. You can wear very nice clothes, if that's your style, but flashy is out.

TIP 5: ALWAYS BRING YOUR MAIN WITNESS TO COURT BEFORE THE TRIAL.

This is so you can walk them through the court, have them sit at the witness stand and at the counsel table, and just generally get a feel for the room. When they're more comfortable with the place, they'll be less likely to make mistakes.

TIP 6: BE POLITICALLY CORRECT AT ALL TIMES.

Never refer to a child as a kid, and never call a client an ex-husband/wife until the divorce is over. Judges hate it when you say "their ex" in the middle of a divorce proceeding. They are not an 'ex' anything until the judgment is entered and they are actually divorced.

TIP 7: BE CIVIL AT ALL TIMES TO THE JUDGE.

This goes without saying. Forever and for all time.

TIP 8: ALWAYS BE CIVIL TO OPPOSING COUNSEL.

What you do in court is your job. What you do outside can defeat your reputation. Job number one is to be nice to opposing counsel. It is also critical to be respectful, but be careful that you're not being a push over. You have to be able to draw lines. You have to be able to put your foot down without swearing or throwing a tantrum.

TIP 9: FOLLOW THE COURT RULES.

These are there for a reason: the effective and efficient dispensation of justice. If you are always late, you will always be playing catch up.

TIP 10: FOCUS ON THE WORK, AND THE MONEY WILL TAKE CARE OF ITSELF.

This is the Zen of law practice.

TIP 11: BE NICE TO EVERYONE.

Karma is real. Be nice to everyone and kill them with kindness instead of insults. Your reputation is worth a king's ransom. Treat it as such.

TIP 12: STAMP JUDGE'S COPY IF YOU ARE TURNING IN A PAPER

There really is no such thing as over-doing anything when it comes to court. Many courts require a copy that is stamped Judges Copy and the ones that do not, it would never hurt.

TIP 13: SEND HOLIDAY CARDS.

Send some sort of holiday card to everyone you know. It brings warm feelings and a guarantee of goodwill that turns into business.

TIP 14: DON'T BE AFRAID TO REFER OUT CASES BEYOND YOUR ABILITIES.

You will know what cases these are.

TIP 15: ALWAYS REMEMBER THAT HONESTY IS THE BEST POLICY.

Never make up stuff. The cases you cite must always be accurate. Never lie to anyone, especially a judge.

TIP 16: KEEP A CHANGE OF CLOTHES AT YOUR OFFICE.

I cannot tell you the number of times that an emergency court hearing occurs or, God forbid, one that did not make it into your calendars. You need to have "court-clothes" as they say in Ireland, at the ready.

TIP 17: KEEP AN EXTRA LEGAL PAD AND PEN IN YOUR
BRIEFCASE.

If you don't the day will come when you will have to run to court in a hurry and find yourself without either. This makes you look really unprepared and unprofessional.

TIP 18: WHEN YOU DO AN EMERGENCY EX PARTE MOTION, MAKE
A GENUINE ATTEMPT TO CONTACT THE OTHER SIDE.
JUDGES DO NOT LIKE TRICKS.

The title says it all.

TIP 19: ALWAYS BE 15-30 MINUTES EARLY. PERIOD.

This lets you get the lay of the land for the hearing, the trial, or the day.

TIP 20: PRACTICE IN FRONT OF THE MIRROR.

Practice your motion or argument in front of the mirror. Really. Just like in Law School.

TIP 21: KEEP AT LEAST TWO CALENDARS.

You are required to be at court when a matter is noticed. Do not miss it. Also, the state bar makes you state that you have a calendaring system that guarantees that if one disappears, you have another.

TIP 22: BE OVER POLITE.

Use "your honor" instead of judge. It is the best way for the court staff to see you are one of the good guys.

TIP 23: NEVER INTERRUPT OPPOSING COUNSEL.

Let the judge do it.

TIP 24: NEVER EVER INTERRUPT THE JUDGE.

This also applies to anyone behind the bench, including magistrates and referees.

TIP 25: BE RESPECTFUL TO COURT PERSONNEL.

Always acknowledge court personnel with a "good morning" or "good afternoon. I cannot tell you how often I see lawyers just walk by someone they work with on a daily basis. It is low-rent behavior and beneath you.

TIP 26: MAKE NICE.

I once knew a lawyer who said, "If you don't hate at least one lawyer a year, you're not doing your job." I disagree. Collect friends not enemies. You can't make all lawyers your friend, but it should not be for lack of trying.

TIP 27: HIRE A LEGAL ASSISTANT.

I know you want to use a computer and assorted technology to circumvent the need for anything but a one-person shop, but that limits your growth. Lawyering is a blood sport at times, and the amount of paper and organization you need just to get through the day is nothing short of mind-boggling. A good legal assistant is worth his or her weight in gold.

TIP 28: NEVER PASS UP AN OPPORTUNITY TO KEEP YOUR MOUTH SHUT.

Lawyers like to be the first one to talk, as though the tone and indeed decision of the listener is based on who goes first. This may be true, some of the time, but not always. Take, for example, a young lawyer who rushed in to talk to a prosecutor about his 75-year-old client who had been arrested for drunk driving. Hes client was 2x past the legal limit, and liability was certain. The young lawyer, fresh off of a two-year stint working for a mentor, let the prosecutor speak first at a pre-trial. "You know," the prosecutor said, "I don't figure she will ever get another of these; her husband just died and, well, I am going to reduce it to careless driving (Note: Careless is not even imagined in this scenario)." Had the young lawyer did what so many do, he would have asked for it to be reduced from enhanced drunk driving (super drunk) to a simple drunk driving; many levels more serious than careless.

TIP 29: DON'T LIE.

Does this even need to be mentioned? Never, ever, ever, ever lie to a judge, a client, or opposing counsel. This is a career destroyer. There was once a lawyer who told his client he had filed an appeal when he did not. He lost his license for a full year.

TIP 30: MAKE "WILL ATTEND" YOUR SLOGAN.

When I worked at the big firm, one of the younger lawyers had a sign above his desk that said, "Will not attend." It set the tone of his whole career. He had a "go away" type feel to his office, and he was bound and determined to curmudgeon his way to a full partnership. He never made partner, and I never wondered why.

TIP 31: LEARN HOW TO BREAK BAD NEWS.

Learn to tell your client the bad news without hedging. Look at them straight in the eyes and say, "You are going to lose this if you go to trial," or "the sentencing guidelines say 20 years in prison." Clients respect people who can be straight with them. They will not like it, but doing it is your job. Have you ever wondered who tells the family if a locked-up client tries to commit suicide in a federal holding facility while awaiting trial? You got it, you do. You have to learn to be a master disseminator of bad news.

TIP 32: CHECK, CHECK AND DOUBLE CHECK.

Never assume something is correct or has been taken care of until you've checked it at least thrice. First, make sure the date for the hearing is correct. This does not mean you have to travel over to court to make sure they are sending out the right notices, but it does mean that if you get two different dates, do not assume one is correct over the other. The real rule would be the last date controls, but make sure. One time in my county, a judge left unexpectedly. All his hearings got adjourned, but many of the notices did not say ADJOURNED TO. They just said a new date. In cases like these, you have to call the court or go there to make darn sure which one is right.

TIP 33: SHOW UP.

When a court notice says you and your client must be at something, you must be there. Some counties do not require the defendant to be at the first pretrial, or the divorce client at the scheduling conference. The problem is that the notice says they must attend. It is better to err on the side of belt and suspenders. What would it hurt to have your client there? It will make them part of the process, and that is good for the case and your image as a lawyer who follows the book.

TIP 34: NEVER PUT ANYTHING IN WRITING THAT YOU WILL REGRET.

So many times, people will make you mad, especially lawyers on the other side. You need to learn how to deliberate and think about the anger sent your way and the best way to respond to it. As I say over and over, it is easy to blast back a snide remark. It is even easier to write a tirade to "set the record straight." Big mistake. I should be the last to talk, but I am learning to hold my fire. Remember, an angry response is not only a bad idea, it could be used as ammunition against you some day. Think about the lawyer using it as an exhibit attached to his next motion.

TIP 35: STAY CONNECTED TO YOUR FRIENDS OUTSIDE THE LEGAL COMMUNITY.

The practice of law is an odd practice because you are constantly surrounded by lawyers. If you're not careful, you'll start becoming a lawyer who only hangs out with lawyers. The best of the best are the lawyers who really hang out with people who are not lawyers. First, they provide a really good referral system and are a breath of fresh air, as they talk about things NOT legal related.

TIP 36: DON'T PLAY BIG SHOT.

Learn the names of the courtroom police officers and the custodian. Most people think lawyers think really highly about themselves and look down on other. While that can be true at times, it wouldn't be fair to say always. Some lawyers are just so focused on the case at hand that they forget to pay attention to life. Don't.

TIP 37: NEVER ACT LIKE YOU'RE CERTAIN ABOUT ANYTHING.

The best lawyers keep their ego at bay. Saying things like, "You're probably going to beat me big time," to opposing counsel can also be disarming and can be used to your advantage.

TIP 38: HELP LAWYER FRIENDS FOR FREE IF THEY NEED YOUR SPECIALTY.

I get it that we are a for-profit business, but I was really taken aback when I met with a friend and wills/trust specialist and he wanted to charge me every penny of what he charged someone he did not know and was not in the business.

TIP 39: KEEP PROPER TRACKING OF YOUR TIME.

Keep track of every hour you spend during the day, even on flat fee cases. This way, you know how to track your money, how much you're making and on what.

TIP 40: MAKE FRIENDS WITH OTHER PROFESSIONALS.

Make it a habit of meeting other professionals from other lines of work, CPAs, doctors, economists, and the like. You will be a happy lawyer if you can call someone to chat before you spend the long dollar on an expert. I once had a friend who specialized in medical malpractice because he went to law school next to a medical school and shared a dorm with medical students. He had dozens of medical friends, and, thus, an instant and cheap source of opinions.

TIP 41: KEEP YOUR FILES IN ORDER.

There is nothing more irritating and unprofessional-looking than when a judge asks for something to support an argument and you cannot find it.

TIP 42: REGULARLY READ THE *RULES OF EVIDENCE*.

Keep the *Rules of Evidence* in your briefcase or pocket or on easy access by computer. A judge once told me that he would read this before every trial. I thought that was astounding until I realized they are just a few dozen pages long. It is a great refresher.

TIP 43: DO PRO BONO WORK.

You owe it. You know it.

TIP 44: DON'T BUY NEW BOOKS.

But buy the court rules annotated every year. It is a must.

TIP 45: NEVER GO WITHOUT MALPRACTICE INSURANCE.

When you start practice, the premium is next to nothing because you have no baggage. A lawyer with a dozen years of practice pays more because he or she has a dozen years of clients and cases. You also better know that you will not be able to get certain court-appointed work without a policy. So as not to date this, I can liken the premium for a year's policy to an expensive weekend for two. On year two, it will be more, and so on for the succeeding years, but guess what, it won't matter because you'll be making more and more money.

TIP 46: REMEMBER YOUR LAW SCHOOL PROFESSORS.

This is not a plug. It's just that one of your best sources for references and questions on "how to" are your old professors—and I have news for you, they love to help. The scary professor from back then is now just a nice woman who wants a former student to win. I am constantly asked to write reference letters for old students. I take time on the letters and really push the students who are my favorites. In one letter I wrote to a prospective employer, I put "HIRE THIS WOMAN."

TIP 47: ADVERTISE , BUT DON'T CHEAPEN THE BUSINESS.
I saw billboards in Chicago with women in lingerie and a heading of "Life is short, get a divorce." This is the quintessential "Better Call Saul" approach, and it is cheap and amateurish.

TIP 48: TAKE VACATIONS AND TURN OFF.

TIP 49: TELL ALL THOSE YOU WORK WITH HOW MUCH YOU APPRECIATE THEM. I USE TO WORK WITH A SENIOR PARTNER THAT EVERY DAY WOULD GO TO HIS LEGAL ASSISTANCE DESK AND TELL HER HOW MUCH HE APPRECIATED HER AND HER WORK.

TIP 50: TAKE A BREAK.
I said it before, and I will say it again: No one ever said on their deathbed that they wished they had spent more time at the office.

CHAPTER 22

CLIENT COMES INTO YOUR OFFICE... (PRACTICE ASSIGNMENTS)

Lincoln: "In law it is good policy to never plead what you need not, lest you oblige yourself to prove what you can not." The Collected Works of Abraham Lincoln edited by Roy P. Basler, Volume I, "Letter to Usher F. Linder" (February 20, 1848), p. 453.

The following are actual scenarios I use in a class I teach called: *Transition to Law Practice.* I have found over the years that law school gives students a lot of analytical and problem-solving skills but never adequately teaches them how to apply these.

PRACTICE EXAMPLES: I

1. A client comes into your office with a "personal injury" matter. You listen to his story and learn that he broke his arm in an accident that he caused because he was drunk. He was ticketed for OWI.

2. A client tells you that she wants to get an annulment because she and her husband have only been married for a short time.

3. A client has been denied parenting time under a prior court order. He shows you an order but without the signature of a judge.

4. A client wants to know if he can get a Personal Protection Order (PPO) against his neighbor for 'harassment'. The client says the harassment has to do with the neighbor's son throwing his baseball into the client's yard.

5. A client wants to sue his child's school because the client's child was accused of stealing and was suspended, but was never charged criminally, so it must not have been real.

6. A client wants you to represent him on his OWI case. It is a second offense, and all he wants is to make sure he can drive to and from work as part of the resolution to the case.

7. A client wants to change custody of his nine-year-old son from his ex. The main reason is that his son would rather live with him.

8. A client tells you that the police want to get a statement from her about a bar fight that someone pointed to her starting last night. Your client tells you she was not even there; she was safely home alone watching a movie. Should she make a statement?

9. A client was caught urinating in public, behind a restaurant, and was ticketed for indecent exposure. Can he be placed on the sex offender registry?

10. A client wants to know if the Sex Offender Registry and the Central Registry is the same thing.

11. A client wants to know if the Central Registry is public.

12. A client wants to sue his estranged girlfriend for alienation of affection.

13. A client wants to sue his fiancée for the wedding ring he gave her now that she has called the wedding off.

14. A client with two prior drunk driving offenses has had his license revoked. How and when can he get his license back?

15. A client has a son who was arrested for MIP (Minor in Possession). He just wants to make sure his son does not go to jail. It is a first offense.

16. A client lent a lawn mower to his friend who lives a few blocks away. The friend will now not give it back. The client wants to know how to get it back. Can he just go into the client's garage and get it?

17. A client has a domestic assault charge. Can he go deer hunting while the charge is pending?

18. A client wants to know the difference between a PPO (Personal Protection Order) and a restraining order.

19. A client fell down at a grocery store or fast food place and was not injured but wants to sue for emotional damage.

20. A client charged with drunk driving admits he was drunk but wants to "get out of the ticket," no matter what it costs.

21. A client owes money to a local hospital, and a collection agency constantly calls him at work. Is there any way to stop this?

22. A client knows his girlfriend drives drunk and wants to know if he can put a tracking device on her cell phone so he knows where she is. He tells you she will never know.

23. A client wants to record telephone calls between his wife and her lover. What do you advise?

24. A client wants to know if she can sue her company for defamation for telling her new employer she was a bad employee. She lost her new job because of it.

25. A client wants to clean up his criminal record. He has an OWI from 10 years ago. Can he get that expunged?

26. A client wants to get a CCW (concealed weapon) permit. How does he do it?

27. A client broke up with his girlfriend and wants her half of the rent from the six months she did not pay while they were living together.

28. A client wants to put in her will that her boyfriend should raise her children if she dies. She does not want the children's legal father raising them.

29. An Asian client believes he was fired because of his race. The employer said he was fired because he missed too many days of work. What do you advise him?

30. A client is in the United States illegally. If he is convicted of
    the felony he is charged with, will he get deported?

Is there a common theme? Probably not. The theme is that lawyering is very random at times. What law school teaches is how to spot an issue. This can be a gift, as well as a curse. For example, you tend to use the lawyering tone and analysis to every situation, including to family and friends. The usual conversation becomes a mental process of "get to the point." This is rule number one for clients, not for family: You help clients get to the poin, the correct point.

Number 1 highlights this idea. The client comes into office with a "personal injury" matter. You listen and hear that he broke his arm in an accident that he caused because he was drunk. He was ticketed for OWI.

The case here is not a personal injury case. It is a criminal drunk driving case. The five minutes you spent on the phone as the client explained what happened probably sounded like this: "I was run off the road by this guy, and I hit a tree and ended up in the hospital in traction." Then, the office appointment comes, and you're ready because you have been researching cases about auto injury. The interview starts, and you see a ticket in his hand and begin to wonder why while he tells the story. "Were you ticketed?" you ask. He responds, "Not for causing the accident. It was the other guy's fault." "Then, what was the ticket for?" "Drunk driving—but the accident was clearly not my fault."

STOP THE PRESSES. It does not matter who caused the accident in this scenario because your client will not collect a dime. This is an obvious drunk driving case. The client, by the way, hoping to get free lawyering on the chance that I would sign him up for a big personal injury case that I would get a third of for my fees. This is super similar to the criminally accused client who wants to sue the police for an arrest for whatever reason. The lawyer has to learn to say, "When we finish this criminal case, I will refer you to a civil rights lawyer." It is as though the client wants the criminal case dismissed because his handcuffs were too tight. Not going to happen. Keep your eye on the ball. Clients will control the show if you let them.

Let's examine how a case should be broken down. Look closely at the facts and the questions that should pop out at you from the information you have gathered or presented.

PRACTICE EXAMPLE: II

State v. Gordon Childs

Professor Gordon Childs is a very respected professor at a local university. He is 50 years old. He has a "project" girlfriend who is 30, and they live together. They have a three-year-old poodle (his) and live near downtown Grand Rapids. They have been living together for about a year when the Professor finds out that his girlfriend is a closet "crack" addict. He is brokenhearted and works for months to get her into the right treatment with the right doctors and the right programs. Then the incident happens.

The police report has the following information:

1. On May 1, 2013, the suspect found out that his girlfriend did not report home at the expected time.

2. He called her parents in Muskegon and found that she had been there all evening.

3. The suspect became concerned, as he knew the parents were "drunks," and he feared for his girlfriend's sobriety.

4. The suspect said at the interview at the police station in Muskegon Heights on May 4 that he went to the home of his girlfriend's mother to look for her at about 22:00 hours.

5. The mother, who was visibly intoxicated, according to the suspect, went with him to find her daughter's "drug dealer."

6. When they arrived at the trailer that the drunk mother believed was the dealer's home, the suspect got out of the vehicle and saw a light on in the home. His girlfriend's car was nowhere in the vicinity.

7. Upon knocking on the door, the suspect noticed through the light of the streetlight that his poodle was standing on the couch, obviously distressed.

8. The suspect banged on the door and finally pushed it open to find an elderly woman he described as a "crack-whore" standing there.

9. The suspect yelled at her, and when she did not respond, he began hitting her.

10. When she fell to the ground, he picked up a plastic bucket and hit her across the face.

11. The suspect's girlfriend was not found.

12. The suspect voluntarily appeared at the police station and was interviewed by Sgt. Manning.

13. The suspect was cooperative.

14. No warrant was issued at the station.

15. Miranda was not given, as no custody was attempted in the conference room.

Pending Warrant...

1. What other facts are necessary to write a warrant?

2. What process does the police follow after the interview? Before?

3. What, if any, will be the charges?

4. The suspect does not have a criminal record. Does this matter?

5. The judge is known to hate men who hit "girls."

6. Do you hold a preliminary hearing (or, probable cause hearing?)

7. Who do you call? Do you call your client?

8. What discovery do you need?

9. If the client wants to go to trial, how and what do you prepare?

10. How do you talk with the client? The prosecutor?

CIVIL PRACTICE EXAMPLE: III

Memo: To all students in Transition to Law Practice Class
From: Managing Attorney
Subject: Assignment
Due: First Class Meeting

Bill: Old Mission Brewing Company Dram Shop File-.25 increments at $175.00 per hour

Our client is Old Mission Brewing in Traverse City, Michigan. The client wants to have a tasting room on the Old Mission Peninsula at its hops farm on Swaney Road. There are several wineries on the Peninsula, and they all either sell samples or give away samples of their wine products. Two of the wineries, Chateau Chantal and Two Lads, sell food in limited selections for appetizers.

As for the wineries, there are Township rules that require a certain percentage of the grapes for the wine to be grown right on the Peninsula for it to be called a Peninsula winery. The Brewery wants to open under the same rules as the wineries do, as well as selling and/or furnish alcohol. It has the appropriate permits to grow hops, and its barn, which it plans to also use as a store or pouring room, and currently has 10 acres of hops growing.

Presently, there are no breweries on the Peninsula.

The client wants to know what it will take to do the following:

1. Get a permit to sell and/or give away samples of Old Mission Ale at its hops farm location on the OMP. This will include the ability to sell 6/12/24 packs, as well as fill, on premises, growlers. Do the winery rules regarding the percentage of grapes grown on the Peninsula apply to this situation with hops?

2. What is the company's liability under the dram shop statute pursuant to Michigan law?

3. If the client wants to add food for sale to its beer tastings, does it need a special license, and if so, what steps are necessary, as well as what requirements under the Township or Grand Traverse County?

Assignment:

1. Research and prepare a memorandum outlining and resolving the client's concerns. Remember, we get to yes in this law firm, so I do not want a paper that says it cannot be done unless it is absolutely not do-able. If there are wineries that sell alcohol on the Peninsula, then why not breweries? After all, beer has less alcohol than wine.

2. Prepare a bill for the Brewing Company, complete with hours and a breakdown regarding time spent suitable to send to a client. USE QUARTER HOURS AT $175.00.

Note: There is no page limit, but you must provide a complete answer. Research how memos that cover the issue, highlighting applicable law applied to these unique facts, are presented to a senior partner.

Note: Be extremely careful about asking for clarifications. The partner on a file is extraordinarily busy and has hired you as a motivated, self-starting associate. Asking for clarification can look a lot like questioning the partner's ability to write a precise assignment. I will certainly be available after the fact to help. Your goal is to figure this out. The end.

Note: This is also not a law review article. It is a typical assignment you will get at a firm, and you would be given a week to produce it. Ask yourself this? What is the partner looking for exactly? How can I impress him/her? Will the partner even read this, or is it make-work? Remember the partner wants it done on time, but do not rush. THE PARTNER DOES NOT WANT A PAPER THAT IS QUICK AND WRONG.

CHAPTER 23

LAWYERISMS AND COMMON SENSE

1. Your right to stretch out your arm ends where my face begins.

2. There are three sides to a story: yours, mine, and the one that really happened.

3. What's the difference between a good lawyer and a great lawyer? A good lawyer knows the law very well, and a great lawyer knows the judge very well...

4. If there were no bad people, there would be no good lawyers.

   Charles Dickens

5. This is a court of law, young man, not a court of justice. It's not how innocent you are but how you put your case.

6. "The difference between the right word and the almost-right word is the difference between lightning and a lightning bug."

   Mark Twain

7. "Compromise is the best and cheapest lawyer."

    Robert Louis Stevenson

8. "A jury consists of twelve persons chosen to decide who has the better lawyer."

    Robert Frost

9. "All we know about the new economic world tells us that nations which train engineers will prevail over those which train lawyers. No nation has ever sued its way to greatness. "

    Richard Lamm

10. There is never a deed so foul that something couldn't be said for the guy; that's why there are lawyers.

    Melvin Belli

11. "Lawyers Are": The only persons in whom ignorance of the law is not punished.

    Jeremy Bentham

12. "When you go into court, you are putting your fate into the hands of twelve people who weren't smart enough to get out of jury duty."

    Norm Crosby

13. "Justice is incidental to law and order."

    John Edgar Hoover

14. "Somebody recently figured out that we have 35 million laws to enforce the Ten Commandments."

    Attributed to both Bert Masterson and Earl Wilson

15. "In the Halls of Justice, the only justice is in the halls."

Lenny Bruce

16. "Although the legal and ethical definitions of right are the antithesis of each other, most writers use them as synonyms. They confuse power with goodness and mistake law for justice."

Charles T. Sprading, Freedom and its Fundamentals

17. "Law never made men a whit more just."

Henry David Thoreau

18. "The United States is a nation of laws badly written and randomly enforced."

Frank Zappa

19. "There is no such thing as justice — in or out of court."

Clarence Darrow

20. "I keep six honest serving-men:
    (They taught me all I knew)
    Their names are What and Where and When
    And How and Why and Who."

Rudyard Kipling

21. "The life of the law has not been logic; it has been experience."

Oliver Wendell Holmes

22. "There's always room for a good lawyer."

Milas Hale

23. "If you want peace, work for justice"

Pope Paul VI

24. "Law is the embodiment of the moral sentiment of the people."

William Blackstone

25. "A man who is his own lawyer has a fool for a client."

Early-19th century proverb found in Henry Kett's
The flowers of wit, or a choice collection of bon mots (1814)

26. "I think the first duty of society is justice."

Alexander Hamilton

27. "Tact is the ability to describe others as they see themselves."

Abraham Lincoln

28. "When it wishes anything done which is really serious, it collects twelve of the ordinary men standing round. The same thing was done, if I remember right, by the Founder of Christianity."

G. K. Chesterton, speaking of society

29. "It may be true that the law cannot make a man love me, but it can stop him from lynching me, and I think that's pretty important."

Martin Luther King, Jr.

30. "Very few souls are saved after the first five minutes of the sermon."

Mark Twain

31. *The Best Advice Is to Use Your Common Sense.*

32. *Advice from an Old Farmer*

Your fences need to be horse-high, pig-tight and bull-strong.

Keep skunks and bankers at a distance.

Life is simpler when you plow around the stump.

A bumblebee is considerably faster than a John Deere tractor.

Words that soak into your ears are whispered... not yelled.

Meanness don't jes' happen overnight.

Forgive your enemies; it messes up their heads.

Do not corner something that you know is meaner than you.

It doesn't take a very big person to carry a grudge.

You cannot unsay a cruel word.

Every path has a few puddles.

When you wallow with pigs, expect to get dirty.

The best sermons are lived, not preached.

Most of the stuff people worry about ain't never gonna happen
anyway.

Don't judge folks by their relatives.

Remember that silence is sometimes the best answer.

Live a good, honorable life... Then when you get older and think back,
you'll enjoy it a second time.

Don't interfere with somethin' that ain't bothering you none.

Timing has a lot to do with the outcome of a Rain dance.

If you find yourself in a hole, the first thing to do is stop diggin'.

Sometimes you get, and sometimes you get got.

The biggest troublemaker you'll probably ever have to deal with
watches you from the mirror every mornin'.

Always drink upstream from the herd.

Good judgment comes from experience, and a lotta that comes
from bad judgment.

Lettin' the cat outta the bag is a whole lot easier
than puttin' it back in.

If you get to thinkin' you're a person of some influence, try orderin'
somebody else's dog around.

Live simply. Love generously. Care deeply. Speak kindly.
Leave the rest to God.
Don't pick a fight with an old man. If he is too old to fight,
he'll just kill you.
Most times, it just gets down to common sense.

33. *Advice from an Old Woman*:

An old woman walked up and tied her old mule to the hitching post. As she stood there, brushing some of the dust from her face and clothes, a young gunslinger stepped out of the saloon with a gun in one hand and a bottle of whiskey in the other. The young gunslinger looked at the old woman and laughed, "Hey old woman, have you ever danced?"

The old woman looked up at the gunslinger and said, "No... I never did dance... Never really wanted to."

A crowd had gathered as the gunslinger grinned and said, "Well, you old bag, you're gonna dance now," and he started shooting at the old woman's feet.

The old woman prospector -- not wanting to get her toe blown off --started hopping around. Everybody was laughing. When his last bullet had been fired, the young gunslinger, still laughing, holstered his gun and turned around to go back into the saloon.

The old woman turned to her pack mule, pulled out a double-barreled shotgun, and cocked both hammers. The loud clicks carried clearly through the desert air, and the crowd stopped laughing immediately.

The young gunslinger heard the sounds, too, and he turned around very slowly. The silence was almost deafening. The crowd watched as the young gunman stared at the old woman and the large gaping holes of those twin barrels.

The barrels of the shotgun never wavered in the old woman's hands as she quietly said, "Son, have you ever kissed a mule's hind end?"

The gunslinger swallowed hard and said, "No ma'am... But I've always wanted to."

THERE ARE A FEW LESSONS HERE FOR ALL OF US:

1 - Never be arrogant.
2 - Don't waste ammunition.
3 - Whiskey makes you think you're smarter than you are.
4 - Always make sure you know who has the power.
5 - Don't mess with old women; they didn't get old by being stupid.

CHAPTER 24

LANNY

No one's life as a lawyer is ever complete without the people who mold and shape them into the lawyer them will become. These people, whether inadvertently or completely on purpose, can turn into lifelines for you and your career. Everyone has a favorite professor story from law school, but you will find that your favorite stories will be from your clients, and especially from those special people called mentors.

At the lake, as they say, I live next door to a lawyer who has practiced for over 50 years. He comes from a county in Michigan where, at a lawyer's passing, they have a hearing and a motion to recognize his life and accomplishments as a practicing attorney, a member in good standing of the bar. Abraham Lincoln called the practice of law: An Honest Calling. Indeed, it is an honest calling. He believed it was more of a calling than a vocation. He also believed it was that thing you did that paid the bills while you were working on the true passion in your life, like politics.

My neighbor is passionate about the practice of law. He is nearly 80 years old and lives permanently where I vacation. Promptly at 8:30 every weekday morning, I hear his garage door open. If you look out the window, you will see him in a sports coat and tie walking to his car with a brisk walk that has kept him fit for his age. He sees going to work every morning, like he has done for 50 years, not as drudgery but a dream come true. To fight for the little guy and the oppressed is his passion. Just give him a case where some young man was soaping the windows of a house or breaking a window and he will tell the prosecutor that his client was just 'being a kid.' He will then break into the obligatory "I remember when I was a kid," story.

His name is Keith, but people, for some reason, call him Lanny. He is all about fairness and has a genuine belief that we lawyers matter. "Can you believe what a gift we have been given to be a lawyer? To take a problem that is causing a family to break or a child to go off to prison and solve it to the good is a remarkable service to humanity." He really believes this.

He practiced law in a small three-person firm that was probably called a three-man firm for most of his career. He was the go-to-guy in his county. He represented banks and car dealers and became as good-ole-boy as you can become in a town of less than 100,000. His practice was very successful. He bought the building he practiced in for 40 years and then rented rooms to younger lawyers. It is a model that is repeated and repeated all over the country and probably all over the world. It is called a loose affiliation or loose partnership. What this means is you are on your own financially; you eat what you kill, but you share expenses.

This is my dream for you or any new lawyer wanting to begin the path to shingle-hood. Sharing is gold when you share with someone like Lanny. To this day, we occasionally sit and have a beer and talk shop, lawyers talk shop. It is just something people like him do. You, of course, never talk about court with a judge when you see her at lunch. Your best bet is to talk to other lawyers, and there are a lot who will talk your ear off. That is what we do. We talk. We also know it all. And, therein, as they say, lies the rub. Learn to listen like Lanny. He is a listener. He is a tireless advocate bent on seeing government as the intruder, the great disrupter. Strange coming from a guy who represented banks. Maybe he had a passion for the little guy, and when he 'so-called' retired, he decided to turn to the other side: the accused.

He will tell stories of his victories, but not because he is bragging, no, not one iota. He will tell about the people he helped. He treats helping as something delicious. He talks about it as righting the wrong pages. There has to be someone to give voice to the mute. "Court is a jungle," he will say. "It is no place for the defenseless." He is now the defender. There is an old saying that a new lawyer gives you a million dollars' worth of work for a dollar and a senior lawyer gives you a dollar's worth of work for a million dollars. Well, not with Lanny. You get a senior lawyer with 50+ years of experience for a dollar. I would say it would be a dollar well spent.

He is what we call in the business a true believer. His heart is in every case, and he respects all those who hire him. He is a master mitigator and solutionist. There is always middle ground for him—but not until he has covered the case from soup to nuts. He is a due diligence type lawyer who will agree that the party is dead and the cause seems obvious, but he will exhaust resources prodding and probing until he finally cries "uncle." Then and only then will he say, "I lose. My client caused the death." Now, on to the mitigation phase.

Remember the old story about the goat:

The plaintiff, a farmer who grew a patch of cabbages behind his house, had a neighbor who kept a goat in his backyard. One day, the goat broke loose, got into the cabbage patch, and ate lots of cabbages while digging up and ruining the rest of the patch. The farmer sued the owner of the goat for his lost cabbages. Here is how the 'raise-every-issue defense lawyer' responded in his opening statement:

'You had no cabbages.
'If you had any cabbages, they were not eaten.
'If your cabbages were eaten, it was not by a goat.
'If your cabbages were eaten by a goat, it wasn't my goat.
And if it was my goat, he was insane at the time.

This is Lanny. He holds on like an old bulldog, but never at the expense of belittling the opposing side. He respects judges and is a champion for the law as a noble trade. His life revolved around mutual benefit, and he would take an old used hot tub for fair trade. He was a barterer. Even if you had no money, you had talent, and you could be the guy fixing the doors at his home. He let the law become his passion.

He often comes over to my house and sits on the deck with me while we drink a beer. I would then prattle on about this case and that case. He is the one with passion for this business, not I. After years of listening to his war stories, and seeing him listening to mine, I found that passion comes in many forms. Lanny has a genuine and obvious passion for unraveling the seemingly unravel-able.

And as he gets up to leave after our latest session of legal tales, he always says, "But that's what we do."

Indeed, my friend, that's what we do.

There Is Nothing Like a Mentor

Rob Swartz rented me space in his office, guidance in the practice of law, and time in his life. He taught me that there is a way to practice law with a belt instead of belt and suspenders. More importantly, he taught me all I know about 'hanging out a shingle.' Today, he will gladly tell anyone who will listen: "I taught him everything he knows." He will then pause, smile, and finish: "just not everything I know." Thanks Rob.

YOU'VE GOT EVERYTHING I KNOW.

www.ingramcontent.com/pod-product-compliance
Lightning Source LLC
Chambersburg PA
CBHW061220220326
41599CB00025B/4705